Eternal life

GOING BEYOND THE BASICS OF REPENTANCE: SOLID FOOD

Lorenzo Hill

COPYRIGHT

Table of Contents

Dedicated To
Our Lord and Saviour
Jesus the Christ of Nazareth

JOHN 10:27-29 KING JAMES VERSION (KJV)

27 My sheep hear my voice, and I know them, and they follow me:
28 And I give unto them eternal life; and they shall never perish, neither shall any man pluck them out of my hand.
29 My Father, which gave them me, is greater than all; and no man is able to pluck them out of my Father's hand.

JOHN 6:53-55 KING JAMES VERSION (KJV)

53 Then Jesus said unto them, Verily, verily, I say unto you, Except ye eat the flesh of the Son of man, and drink his blood, ye have no life in you.
54 Whoso eateth my flesh, and drinketh my blood, hath eternal life; and I will raise him up at the last day.
55 For my flesh is meat indeed, and my blood is drink indeed.

JOHN 17:1-3 KING JAMES VERSION (KJV)

17 These words spake Jesus, and lifted up his eyes to heaven, and said, Father, the hour is come; glorify thy Son, that thy Son also may glorify thee:
2 As thou hast given him power over all flesh, that he should give eternal life to as many as thou hast given him.
3 And this is life eternal, that they might know thee the only true God, and Jesus Christ, whom thou hast sent.

CHAPTER 1

What Is Eternal Life

Since the beginning of time man has been exposed to the concept of eternal life. We are told in the book of Genesis that one of the reasons Adam and Eve were expelled from the Garden was so they would not eat of the tree of life.

GENESIS 2:8-9 KING JAMES VERSION (KJV)[1]

8 And the Lord God planted a garden eastward in Eden; and there he put the man whom he had formed.

9 And out of the ground made the Lord God to grow every tree that is pleasant to the sight, and good for food; the tree of life also in the midst of the garden, and the tree of knowledge of good and evil.

GENESIS 3:21-23 AMPLIFIED BIBLE (AMP)

21 The Lord God made tunics of [animal] skins for Adam and his wife and clothed them.

22 And the Lord God said, "Behold, the man has become like one of Us (Father, Son, Holy Spirit), knowing [how to distinguish between] good and evil; and now, he might stretch out his hand, and take from the tree of life as well, and eat [its fruit], and live [in this fallen, sinful condition] forever"—

23 therefore the Lord God sent Adam away from the Garden of Eden, to till and cultivate the ground from which he was taken.

---

[1] All quotes from the King James Version (KJV) and the Amplified bibles were taken from the site www.biblegateway.com. All King James Bible quotes are from a Public Domain version. See copyright page for Amplified copyright permissions.

GENESIS 3:21-23 KING JAMES VERSION (KJV)
[21] Unto Adam also and to his wife did the Lord God make coats of skins, and clothed them.
[22] And the Lord God said, Behold, the man is become as one of us, to know good and evil: and now, lest he put forth his hand, and take also of the tree of life, and eat, and live for ever:
[23] Therefore the Lord God sent him forth from the garden of Eden, to till the ground from whence he was taken.

Here we can see from the very beginning in the scripture we are exposed to the concept of Eternal Life. Man has been seeking this in various ways all throughout time. We have heard of those who seek the fountain of youth and many other tales from different religions and traditions and sources. Some believe in reincarnation while others just want to retain youth. Each of these is rooted in a desire to never die. We see today how the Egyptians mummified bodies in hope of them lasting forever. Even today there are many rich and famous people who try to preserve their bodies hoping that one day in the future man will discover cures for their ailments so that may have eternal life. Some have gone as far as to have themselves frozen in nitrogen to preserve their bodies so that they can be revived in the future when medicine finds a way to heal their ailments and prolong their existence. Most of these efforts are so that they who consider themselves more valued and more relevant than the common person might be preserved to continue to control wealth and power.

Some adhere to the thought that there is no life beyond this so why worry about anything beyond this life. To many, eternal life is also tied into our moral structure. Paul states this in scripture.

1 Corinthians 15:31-37 KING James Version (KJV)
[31] I protest by your rejoicing which I have in Christ Jesus our Lord, I die daily.
[32] If after the manner of men I have fought with beasts at Ephesus, what advantageth it me, if the dead rise not? let us eat and drink; for to morrow we die.
[33] Be not deceived: evil communications corrupt good manners.
[34] Awake to righteousness, and sin not; for some have not the knowledge of God: I speak this to your shame.
[35] But some man will say, How are the dead raised up? and with what body do they come?
[36] Thou fool, that which thou sowest is not quickened, except it die:

37 And that which thou sowest, thou sowest not that body that shall be, but bare grain, it may chance of wheat, or of some other grain:
1 CORINTHIANS 15:31-37 AMPLIFIED BIBLE (AMP)
31 I assure you, believers, by the pride which I have in you in [your union with] Christ Jesus our Lord, I die daily [I face death and die to self].
32 What good has it done me if, [merely] from a human point of view, I [a]fought with wild animals at Ephesus? If the dead are not raised [at all], let us eat and drink [enjoying ourselves now], for tomorrow we die.
33 Do not be deceived: [b]"Bad company corrupts good morals."
34 Be sober-minded [be sensible, wake up from your spiritual stupor] as you ought, and stop sinning; for some [of you] have no knowledge of God [you are disgracefully ignorant of Him, and ignore His truths]. I say this to your shame.
35 But someone will say, "How are the dead raised? And with what kind of body will they come?"
36 You fool! Every time you plant seed you sow something that does not come to life [germinating, springing up and growing] unless it first dies.
37 The seed you sow is not the body (the plant) which it is going to become, but it is a bare seed, perhaps of wheat or some other grain.
Footnotes:
1 Corinthians 15:32 This may refer figuratively to the furious crowd that rose up against Paul in Ephesus, rather than to literal animals (Acts 19:23-41).
1 Corinthians 15:33 Paul quotes this one verse maxim from the writings of the Greek dramatist Menander (342-291 b.c.). "Bad company" in this case undoubtedly refers to the teachers who were denying the truth of the resurrection.

Those who feel that death is the end and there is nothing beyond this life have no reason to live, other than to get the most they can from this life in self-indulgent pleasure without regard to anything or anyone else. Our view on whether eternal life is real has a big bearing on how we choose to live our lives. Those without hope live in accordance with their own established principles because they see no need for anything else. To them, truth is what they perceive it to be and nothing else. Their truth is the world revolves around them and they are all that matters. Therefore, why should they be concerned with right and wrong? What they choose to be right to them is their truth. They just live with those things they find comforting. Their ideals and their self-worth are all that are important. For them, there is no God nor is there any creator, just happenstance and man's own wit or intelligence. Yes, as the apostle Paul states, "without a hope in the resurrection why do anything other than to live for the here and now?"

LUKE 16:10-15 KING JAMES VERSION (KJV)

10 He that is faithful in that which is least is faithful also in much: and he that is unjust in the least is unjust also in much.

11 If therefore ye have not been faithful in the unrighteous mammon, who will commit to your trust the true riches?

12 And if ye have not been faithful in that which is another man's, who shall give you that which is your own?

13 No servant can serve two masters: for either he will hate the one, and love the other; or else he will hold to the one, and despise the other. Ye cannot serve God and mammon.

14 And the Pharisees also, who were covetous, heard all these things: and they derided him.

15 And he said unto them, Ye are they which justify yourselves before men; but God knoweth your hearts: for that which is highly esteemed among men is abomination in the sight of God.

So, here is the first part of what eternal life is according to scripture. Eternal life is a driver of our moral structure. Some seek it through Satanic and other sources, but what does the bible have to say about it? We cling to this life because to us, it is the only existence, we are sure of and that we can prove using our senses. So many of us will do all that we can to hold onto this life as long as we can. We are driven by our senses. If we can't see, touch, feel, or smell it, then it is not real. Can we see, smell or taste our thoughts or our reasoning powers? What we know is our present state. So, this is what we are naturally bound to cling or hold on to. We will accept whatever seems logical to us. Many have been duped by so-called spiritualist or those who claim to have contact with the dead. Yes, some of these do have contact with evil spirits, but not in the way most believe. Some try to get us to believe that we all have eternal life, but even this is a false representation of the truth. So, many buy into those things which at the time seem most plausible or believable or acceptable.

2 CORINTHIANS 4:17-18 KING JAMES VERSION (KJV)

17 For our light affliction, which is but for a moment, worketh for us a far more exceeding and eternal weight of glory;

[18] While we look not at the things which are seen, but at the things which are not seen: for the things which are seen are temporal; but the things which are not seen are eternal.

Next, in Genesis as quoted earlier eternal life is derived by partaking of a fruit from a tree, just as we obtained the knowledge of good and evil. We will get into this more later, but the fruit is the work of God and the tree is Jesus the Christ.

Third, is the fact that eternal life or eternal existence has to do with a life that continues beyond death as we know it. As mentioned above, man has his own ideas about eternal life some are even close to the scriptural account, but my task is only to approach this only from the scriptural perspective. The best way to understand the truth is to know what is written in scripture, rather than studying the false which only confuses your knowledge. Then you will be able to spot the false or counterfeit items readily.

Now how does scripture define eternal life? I am led to point you to the scriptures below.

PROVERBS 12:28 AMPLIFIED BIBLE (AMP)

[28] In the way of righteousness is life, And in its pathway there is no death [but immortality—eternal life].

MATTHEW 25:45-46 AMPLIFIED BIBLE (AMP)

[45] Then He will reply to them, 'I assure you and most solemnly say to you, to the extent that you did not do it for one of the least of these [my followers], you did not do it for Me.'

[46] Then these [unbelieving people] will go away into eternal (unending) punishment, but those who are righteous and in right standing with God [will go, by His remarkable grace] into eternal (unending) life."

MATTHEW 25:45-46 KING JAMES VERSION (KJV)

[45] Then shall he answer them, saying, Verily I say unto you, Inasmuch as ye did it not to one of the least of these, ye did it not to me.

[46] And these shall go away into everlasting punishment: but the righteous into life eternal.

JOHN 3:16-19 AMPLIFIED BIBLE (AMP)

[16] "For God so [greatly] loved and dearly prized the world, that He [even] gave His [One and] [a]only begotten Son, so that whoever believes and trusts in Him [as Savior] shall not perish, but have eternal life.

[17] *For God did not send the Son into the world to judge and condemn the world [that is, to initiate the final judgment of the world], but that the world might be saved through Him.*

[18] *Whoever believes and has decided to trust in Him [as personal Savior and Lord] is not judged [for this one, there is no judgment, no rejection, no condemnation]; but the one who does not believe [and has decided to reject Him as personal Savior and Lord] is judged already [that one has been convicted and sentenced], because [b]he has not believed and trusted in the name of the [One and] only begotten Son of God [the One who is truly unique, the only One of His kind, the One who alone can save him].*

[19] *This is the judgment [that is, the cause for indictment, the test by which people are judged, the basis for the sentence]: the Light has come into the world, and people loved the [c]darkness rather than the Light, for their deeds were evil.*

Footnotes:

John 3:16 Jesus, God's only Son, the One who is truly unique, the only one of His kind.

John 3:18 The Greek refers to an unsaved person who has made the decision not to believe in the Son, Jesus Christ, that is, not to accept the salvation offered by the Son and commit to follow Him. Such a person stands condemned by God unless he changes his mind.

John 3:19 See note 1:5.

JOHN 1:5 AMPLIFIED BIBLE (AMP)

[5] *The Light shines on in the [a]darkness, and the darkness did not understand it or overpower it or appropriate it or absorb it [and is unreceptive to it].*

Footnotes:

John 1:5 I.e. the world immersed in sin: all that stands in opposition to God and biblical truth.

JOHN 3:35-36 AMPLIFIED BIBLE (AMP)

[35] *The Father loves the Son and has given and entrusted all things into His hand.*

[36] *He who believes and trusts in the Son and accepts Him [as Savior] has eternal life [that is, already possesses it]; but he who does not believe the Son and chooses to reject Him, [disobeying Him and denying Him as Savior] will not see [eternal] life, but [instead] the wrath of God hangs over him continually."*

JOHN 4:9-14 AMPLIFIED BIBLE (AMP)

[9] *The Samaritan woman asked Him, "How is it that You, being a Jew, ask me, a [a]Samaritan woman, for a drink?" (For Jews have nothing to do with Samaritans.)*

[10] Jesus answered her, "If you knew [about] God's gift [of eternal life], and who it is who says, 'Give Me a drink,' you would have asked Him [instead], and He would have given you living water (eternal life)."

[11] She said to Him, "Sir, [b]You have nothing to draw with [no bucket and rope] and the well is deep. Where then do You get that living water?

[12] Are You greater than our father [c]Jacob, who gave us the well, and who used to drink from it himself, and his sons and his cattle also?"

[13] Jesus answered her, "Everyone who drinks this water will be thirsty again.

[14] But whoever drinks the water that I give him will never be thirsty again. But the water that I give him will become in him a spring of water [satisfying his thirst for God] welling up [continually flowing, bubbling within him] to eternal life."

Footnotes:

John 4:9 The Jews considered Samaritan women ceremonially unclean.

John 4:11 The woman's response is due to the fact that "living water" was the normal description for running water. She probably thought that Jesus was referring to the underground water source that fed the well.

John 4:12 Jacob (renamed Israel in Gen 32:28) was the son of Isaac, grandson of Abraham and father of the twelve sons who established the twelve tribes of Israel.

Footnotes:

JOHN 5:23-25 AMPLIFIED BIBLE (AMP)

[23] so that all will give honor (reverence, homage) to the Son just as they give honor to the Father. [In fact] the one who does not honor the Son does not honor the Father who has sent Him.

[24] "I assure you and most solemnly say to you, the person who hears My word [the one who heeds My message], and believes and trusts in Him who sent Me, has (possesses now) eternal life [that is, eternal life actually begins—the believer is transformed], and does not come into judgment and condemnation, but has passed [over] from death into life.

Two Resurrections

[25] I assure you and most solemnly say to you, a time is coming and is [here] now, when the dead will hear the voice of the Son of God, and those who hear it will live.

PSALM 49:8-10 AMPLIFIED BIBLE (AMP)

[8] For the ransom of his soul is too costly, And he should cease trying forever—

[9] So that he should live on eternally, That he should never see the pit (grave) and undergo decay.

[10] For he sees that even wise men die; The fool and the stupid alike perish And leave their wealth to others.

JOHN 6:67-69 KING JAMES VERSION (KJV)

[67] Then said Jesus unto the twelve, Will ye also go away?

[68] Then Simon Peter answered him, Lord, to whom shall we go? thou hast the words of eternal life.

[69] And we believe and are sure that thou art that Christ, the Son of the living God.

JOHN 10:27-29 KING JAMES VERSION (KJV)

[27] My sheep hear my voice, and I know them, and they follow me:

[28] And I give unto them eternal life; and they shall never perish, neither shall any man pluck them out of my hand.

[29] My Father, which gave them me, is greater than all; and no man is able to pluck them out of my Father's hand.

JOHN 17:2-4 KING JAMES VERSION (KJV)

[2] As thou hast given him power over all flesh, that he should give eternal life to as many as thou hast given him.

[3] And this is life eternal, that they might know thee the only true God, and Jesus Christ, whom thou hast sent.

[4] I have glorified thee on the earth: I have finished the work which thou gavest me to do.

JOHN 17:2-4 AMPLIFIED BIBLE (AMP)

[2] Just as You have given Him power and authority over all mankind, [now glorify Him] so that He may give eternal life [a]to all whom You have given Him [to be His—permanently and forever].

[3] Now this is eternal life: that they may know You, the only true [supreme and sovereign] God, and [in the same manner know] Jesus [as the] Christ whom You have sent.

[4] I have glorified You [down here] on the earth by [b]completing the work that You gave Me to do.

Footnotes:

John 17:2 A reference to election or predestination. Also see John 6:39; 17:6, 9, 24; Acts 13:48; Rom 8:29-33; Eph 1:3-6; 2 Thess 2:13; 1 Pet 1:2.

John 17:4 Much of Jesus' discourse and prayer in John 13-17 is reminiscent of God's comparison of rain and snow to His word in Is 55:10, 11. Like God's word, Jesus, who was introduced by John as the Word (John 1:1), comes from God (John 16:28; 17:8), accomplishes God's desire (John 14:10; 17:4, 8) and then returns to God (John 13:33; 14:4; 17:13).The themes of joy and peace found in Isaiah 55:12 also resonate throughout John 13-17; joy (John 15:11; 16:20-24; 17:13) and peace (John 14:27; 16:33). Isaiah 55; 56 has many points of connection with John's Gospel as a whole, most notably the invitations to quench thirst (Is 55:1; John 4:13, 14; 7:37) and receive bread (Is 55:2; John 6:26-35, 48-51). Other points of connection between Is 55; 56 and John include the tie between listening and living, appeals to witnesses, calls to obedience, the idea of a special window of God's nearness, and the inclusion of the Gentiles in salvation.

Here we see that eternal life is not just the knowledge of Jesus as the Son and God as the Father but the full acceptance of them and their ways. These scriptures are in essence saying we are to accept them in order for us to experience eternal life. For many, this is hard to grasp. It is an essential part of the gospel that we must accept them in their respective roles before we can acquire this gift. Yes, it is vital to receive them both, otherwise there is nothing. Because in order for eternal life to be real we must except the fact someone has prepared it, assures it and sustains it. This is because what we accept now and what we see without this is death is the end to all existence. This is why we have such a great fear of death. So, we need a hope and an assurance beyond ourselves and this is brought about through our acceptance of the first eternal beings, God the Father and His Son Christ Jesus of Nazareth. Hence, we gain proof of eternal life through this knowledge. Even though it is at this present time not yet visible, the assurance lies in the resurrection of the Son and the many on the day of Christ's resurrection. Our response to this is our obedience to His commandments and a lifestyle which supports these truths.

2 CORINTHIANS 5:1-3 KING JAMES VERSION (KJV)

¹ For we know that if our earthly house of this tabernacle were dissolved, we have a building of God, an house not made with hands, eternal in the heavens.

² For in this we groan, earnestly desiring to be clothed upon with our house which is from heaven:

³ If so be that being clothed we shall not be found naked.

EZEKIEL 37:12-14 AMPLIFIED BIBLE (AMP)

¹² Therefore prophesy and say to them, 'Thus says the Lord God, "Behold, I will open your graves and make you come up out of your graves, My people; and I will bring you [back home] to the land of Israel.

¹³ Then you will know [with confidence] that I am the Lord, when I have opened your graves and made you come up out of your graves, My people.

¹⁴ I will put My [a]Spirit in you and you will come to life, and I will place you in your own land. Then you will know that I the Lord have spoken, and fulfilled it," says the Lord.'"

MATTHEW 27:52-54 AMPLIFIED BIBLE (AMP)

⁵² The tombs were opened, and many bodies of the saints (God's people) who had fallen asleep [in death] were raised [to life];

⁵³ and coming out of the tombs after His resurrection, they entered the holy city (Jerusalem) and appeared to many people.

⁵⁴ Now the centurion, and those who were with him keeping guard over Jesus, when they saw the earthquake and the things that were happening, they were terribly frightened and filled with awe, and said, "Truly this was the Son of God!"

God has sent his heralds to announce the truth of existence beyond this life so that we will have something tangible to hold on to. Just as the talk shows have someone who stands before them to introduce them, God has sent His messengers to proclaim that which we need to know to have a hope in what we haven't seen or experienced in this life. They provide for us a vision of what is about to occur so that our anticipation is peeked to its upmost, giving us a view of what we can expect in our future.

TITUS 1:1-3 KING JAMES VERSION (KJV)

¹ Paul, a servant of God, and an apostle of Jesus Christ, according to the faith of God's elect, and the acknowledging of the truth which is after godliness;

² In hope of eternal life, which God, that cannot lie, promised before the world began;

³ But hath in due times manifested his word through preaching, which is committed unto me according to the commandment of God our Saviour;

HEBREWS 9:14-16 KING JAMES VERSION (KJV)

¹⁴ How much more shall the blood of Christ, who through the eternal Spirit offered himself without spot to God, purge your conscience from dead works to serve the living God?

¹⁵ And for this cause he is the mediator of the new testament, that by means of death, for the redemption of the transgressions that were under the first testament, they which are called might receive the promise of eternal inheritance.

16 For where a testament is, there must also of necessity be the death of the testator.

1 JOHN 5:10-12 KING JAMES VERSION (KJV)

10 He that believeth on the Son of God hath the witness in himself: he that believeth not God hath made him a liar; because he believeth not the record that God gave of his Son.

11 And this is the record, that God hath given to us eternal life, and this life is in his Son.

12 He that hath the Son hath life; and he that hath not the Son of God hath not life.

From the scripture above we see that Eternal life is not a place, but a state of existence which goes beyond our physical death. Even though our bodies die and decay, the portion of us which is spirit will live on for forever and at some point, in time, it will be reunited with our bodies and we will live on eternally with God in both body and spirit. It is a state that God has granted us to be with Him and Christ Jesus. It is granted to those who believe in God and Christ Jesus as a gift not something we earn. We are justified by following God's commandments. We, through our actions, demonstrate that we have accepted God as the one and only true God and Jesus Christ as our savior. When this act of repentance occurs, we enter into His eternal kingdom along with the gift of the Holy Spirit to transform us into the image of Christ Jesus. It is a point of belief and commitment that we make toward God in response to His offer through Christ Jesus of forgiveness and obedience to His commandments for righteous living. As stated in the previous books which I was inspired to write, repentance is essential as part of our agreement with God. God promises replace our stony hearts with a clean heart and mind so that we can be perfected to be able to dwell with Him and Christ Jesus. This is work, that the Holy Spirit will perform in each of us, based upon our willing cooperation.

Now don't' confuse paradise or heaven with eternal life. Paradise or heaven is a place or a location, not a condition or a state of existence. When mentioned in scripture paradise or heaven is always in reference to visiting a location.

2 CORINTHIANS 12:3-5 KING JAMES VERSION (KJV)
³ And I knew such a man, (whether in the body, or out of the body, I cannot tell: God knoweth;)
⁴ How that he was caught up into paradise, and heard unspeakable words, which it is not lawful for a man to utter.
⁵ Of such an one will I glory: yet of myself I will not glory, but in mine infirmities.

The Spirit calls my attention to one other location which is also described as a state of being. This is Zion. Zion is stated as the place where Enoch and his followers lived which was taken into heaven. It is also stated as being the New Jerusalem and the permanent habitation of God when He returns to earth. Here are a few scriptures which confirm this.

1 KINGS 8:1-3 KING JAMES VERSION (KJV)
¹ Then Solomon assembled the elders of Israel, and all the heads of the tribes, the chief of the fathers of the children of Israel, unto king Solomon in Jerusalem, that they might bring up the ark of the covenant of the Lord out of the city of David, which is Zion.
² And all the men of Israel assembled themselves unto king Solomon at the feast in the month Ethanim, which is the seventh month.
³ And all the elders of Israel came, and the priests took up the ark.

PSALM 87:4-6 KING JAMES VERSION (KJV)
⁴ I will make mention of Rahab and Babylon to them that know me: behold Philistia, and Tyre, with Ethiopia; this man was born there.
⁵ And of Zion it shall be said, This and that man was born in her: and the highest himself shall establish her.
⁶ The Lord shall count, when he writeth up the people, that this man was born there. Selah.

PSALM 132:12-14 KING JAMES VERSION (KJV)
¹² If thy children will keep my covenant and my testimony that I shall teach them, their children shall also sit upon thy throne for evermore.
¹³ For the Lord hath chosen Zion; he hath desired it for his habitation.
¹⁴ This is my rest for ever: here will I dwell; for I have desired it.

ISAIAH 2:2-4 KING JAMES VERSION (KJV)
² And it shall come to pass in the last days, that the mountain of the Lord's house shall be established in the top of the mountains, and shall be exalted above the hills; and all nations shall flow unto it.
³ And many people shall go and say, Come ye, and let us go up to the mountain of the Lord, to the house of the God of Jacob; and he

will teach us of his ways, and we will walk in his paths: for out of Zion shall go forth the law, and the word of the Lord from Jerusalem.

[4] And he shall judge among the nations, and shall rebuke many people: and they shall beat their swords into plowshares, and their spears into pruninghooks: nation shall not lift up sword against nation, neither shall they learn war any more.

ISAIAH 60:13-15 KING JAMES VERSION (KJV)

[13] The glory of Lebanon shall come unto thee, the fir tree, the pine tree, and the box together, to beautify the place of my sanctuary; and I will make the place of my feet glorious.

[14] The sons also of them that afflicted thee shall come bending unto thee; and all they that despised thee shall bow themselves down at the soles of thy feet; and they shall call thee; The city of the Lord, The Zion of the Holy One of Israel.

[15] Whereas thou has been forsaken and hated, so that no man went through thee, I will make thee an eternal excellency, a joy of many generations.

LAMENTATIONS 1:3-5 KING JAMES VERSION (KJV)

[3] Judah is gone into captivity because of affliction, and because of great servitude: she dwelleth among the heathen, she findeth no rest: all her persecutors overtook her between the straits.

[4] The ways of Zion do mourn, because none come to the solemn feasts: all her gates are desolate: her priests sigh, her virgins are afflicted, and she is in bitterness.

[5] Her adversaries are the chief, her enemies prosper; for the Lord hath afflicted her for the multitude of her transgressions: her children are gone into captivity before the enemy.

OBADIAH 20-21 KING JAMES VERSION (KJV)

[20] And the captivity of this host of the children of Israel shall possess that of the Canaanites, even unto Zarephath; and the captivity of Jerusalem, which is in Sepharad, shall possess the cities of the south.

[21] And saviours shall come up on mount Zion to judge the mount of Esau; and the kingdom shall be the Lord's.

ZECHARIAH 2:9-11 KING JAMES VERSION (KJV)

[9] For, behold, I will shake mine hand upon them, and they shall be a spoil to their servants: and ye shall know that the Lord of hosts hath sent me.

[10] Sing and rejoice, O daughter of Zion: for, lo, I come, and I will dwell in the midst of thee, saith the Lord.

[11] And many nations shall be joined to the Lord in that day, and shall be my people: and I will dwell in the midst of thee, and thou shalt know that the Lord of hosts hath sent me unto thee.

HEBREWS 12:21-23 AMPLIFIED BIBLE (AMP)

[21] In fact, so terrifying was the sight, that Moses said, "I am filled with fear and trembling."

[22] But you have come to Mount Zion and to the city of the living God, the heavenly Jerusalem, and to myriads of angels [in festive gathering],

[23] and to the general assembly and assembly of the firstborn who are registered [as citizens] in heaven, and to God, who is Judge of all, and to the spirits of the righteous (the redeemed in heaven) who have been made perfect [bringing them to their final glory],

1 PETER 2:5-7 AMPLIFIED BIBLE (AMP)

[5] You [believers], like living stones, are [a]being built up into a spiritual house for a holy and dedicated priesthood, to offer spiritual sacrifices [that are] acceptable and pleasing to God through Jesus Christ.

[6] For this is contained in Scripture: "Behold, I am laying in Zion a chosen stone, a precious (honored) Cornerstone,

And he who believes in Him [whoever adheres to, trusts in, and relies on Him] will never be disappointed [in his expectations]."

[7] This precious value, then, is for you who believe [in Him as God's only Son—the Source of salvation]; but for those who disbelieve,

"The [very] stone which the builders rejected

Has become the chief Cornerstone,"

Footnotes:

1 Peter 2:5 Or are to be built.

REVELATION 14:1-3 AMPLIFIED BIBLE (AMP)

The Lamb and the 144,000 on Mount Zion

[1] Then I looked, and this is what I saw: the Lamb stood [firmly established] on Mount Zion, and with Him a hundred and forty-four thousand who had His name and His Father's name inscribed on their foreheads [signifying God's own possession].

[2] And I heard a voice from heaven, like the sound of great waters and like the rumbling of mighty thunder; and the voice that I heard [seemed like music and] was like the sound of harpists playing on their harps.

[3] And they sang a new song before the throne [of God] and before the four living creatures and the elders; and no one could learn the song except the hundred and forty-four thousand who had been purchased (ransomed, redeemed) from the earth.

1 NEPHI 3:186-188 THE BOOK OF MORMON

[186] *And in them shall be written my gospel, saith the Lamb, and my rock and my salvation;*

[187] *And blessed are they who shall seek to bring forth my Zion at that day, for they shall have the gift and the power of the Holy Ghost;*

[188] *And if they endure unto the end, they shall be lifted up at the last day, and shall be saved in the everlasting kingdom of the Lamb;*

GENESIS 7:23-34 INSPIRED VERSION

[23] *And the Lord called his people, Zion, because they were of one heart and of one mind, and dwelt in righteousness; and there were no poor among them.*

[24] *And Enoch continued his preaching in righteousness unto the people of God.*

[25] *And it came to pass in his days, that he built a city that was called the city of Holiness, even Zion.*

[26] *And it came to pass, that Enoch talked with the Lord, and he said unto the Lord, Surely, Zion shall dwell in safety forever. But the Lord said unto Enoch, Zion have I blessed, but the residue of the people have I cursed.*

[27] *And it came to pass, that the Lord showed unto Enoch all the inhabitants of the earth, and he beheld, and lo! Zion in process of time was taken up into heaven.*

[28] *And the Lord said unto Enoch, Behold mine abode forever.*

[29] *And Enoch also beheld the residue of the people which were the sons of Adam, and they were a mixture of all the seed of Adam, save it were the seed of Cain; for the seed of Cain were black, and had not place among them.*

[30] *And after that Zion was taken up into heaven, Enoch beheld, and lo, all the nations of the earth were before him; and there came generation upon generation.*

[31] *And Enoch was high and lifted up, even in the bosom of the Father and the Son of Man; and, behold, the powers of Satan were upon all the face of the earth; and he saw angels descending out of heaven, and he heard a loud voice, saying, Woe! woe! be unto the inhabitants of the earth!*

[32] *And he beheld Satan, and he had a great chain in his hand, and it veiled the whole face of the earth with darkness; and he looked up and laughed, and his angels rejoiced.*

[33] *And Enoch beheld angels descending out of heaven, bearing testimony of the Father, and of the Son.*

34 And the Holy Ghost fell on many, and they were caught up by the powers of heaven into Zion.

Summary

Yes, God has provided proof in scripture and through our everyday experiences that there is life after death. Prior to the resurrection of Jesus, we are provided several examples of those who were raised from the dead but they did not have eternal life at that point. We are also told in the scripture that there are those who did not suffer death but were immediately taken to heaven such as Enoch and his followers. The scripture states they were taken and found no more, that is on this earth.

GENESIS 5:21-24 AMPLIFIED BIBLE (AMP)

21 When Enoch was sixty-five years old, he became the father of Methuselah.
22 Enoch walked [in habitual fellowship] with God three hundred years after the birth of Methuselah and had other sons and daughters.
23 So all the days of Enoch were three hundred and sixty-five years.
24 And [in reverent fear and obedience] Enoch walked with God; and he was not [found among men], because God took him [away to be home with Him].

Yes, there are some who did not suffer death in this life, but the rest of us do. Eternal life is something which is provided as a gift through our commitment to believe on Jesus and commit to Him in the waters of baptism for repentance from our sins.

MATTHEW 19:28-30 AMPLIFIED BIBLE (AMP)

28 Jesus said to them, "I assure you and most solemnly say to you, in the renewal [that is, the Messianic restoration and regeneration of all things] when the Son of Man sits on His glorious throne, you [who have followed Me, becoming My disciples] will also sit on twelve thrones, judging the twelve tribes of Israel.
29 And everyone who has left houses or brothers or sisters or father or mother [a]or children or farms for My name's sake will receive many times as much, and will inherit eternal life.
30 But many who are first [in this world] will be last [in the world to come]; and the last, first.
Footnotes:
Matthew 19:29 One early mss adds or wife.

MATTHEW 25:45-46 KING JAMES VERSION (KJV)

[45] *Then shall he answer them, saying, Verily I say unto you, Inasmuch as ye did it not to one of the least of these, ye did it not to me.*

[46] *And these shall go away into everlasting punishment: but the righteous into life eternal.*

JOHN 3:14-16 KING JAMES VERSION (KJV)

[14] *And as Moses lifted up the serpent in the wilderness, even so must the Son of man be lifted up:*

[15] *That whosoever believeth in him should not perish, but have eternal life.*

[16] *For God so loved the world, that he gave his only begotten Son, that whosoever believeth in him should not perish, but have everlasting life.*

JOHN 4:35-37 KING JAMES VERSION (KJV)

[35] *Say not ye, There are yet four months, and then cometh harvest? behold, I say unto you, Lift up your eyes, and look on the fields; for they are white already to harvest.*

[36] *And he that reapeth receiveth wages, and gathereth fruit unto life eternal: that both he that soweth and he that reapeth may rejoice together.*

[37] *And herein is that saying true, One soweth, and another reapeth.*

JOHN 5:38-40 KING JAMES VERSION (KJV)

[38] *And ye have not his word abiding in you: for whom he hath sent, him ye believe not.*

[39] *Search the scriptures; for in them ye think ye have eternal life: and they are they which testify of me.*

[40] *And ye will not come to me, that ye might have life.*

JOHN 6:67-69 KING JAMES VERSION (KJV)

[67] *Then said Jesus unto the twelve, Will ye also go away?*

[68] *Then Simon Peter answered him, Lord, to whom shall we go? thou hast the words of eternal life.*

[69] *And we believe and are sure that thou art that Christ, the Son of the living God.*

JOHN 10:27-29 KING JAMES VERSION (KJV)

[27] *My sheep hear my voice, and I know them, and they follow me:*

[28] *And I give unto them eternal life; and they shall never perish, neither shall any man pluck them out of my hand.*

[29] *My Father, which gave them me, is greater than all; and no man is able to pluck them out of my Father's hand.*

JOHN 10:27-29 KING JAMES VERSION (KJV)

[27] *My sheep hear my voice, and I know them, and they follow me:*

28 And I give unto them eternal life; and they shall never perish, neither shall any man pluck them out of my hand.

29 My Father, which gave them me, is greater than all; and no man is able to pluck them out of my Father's hand.

JOHN 17:1-3 KING JAMES VERSION (KJV)

1 These words spake Jesus, and lifted up his eyes to heaven, and said, Father, the hour is come; glorify thy Son, that thy Son also may glorify thee:

2 As thou hast given him power over all flesh, that he should give eternal life to as many as thou hast given him.

3 And this is life eternal, that they might know thee the only true God, and Jesus Christ, whom thou hast sent.

JUDE 20-22 KING JAMES VERSION (KJV)

20 But ye, beloved, building up yourselves on your most holy faith, praying in the Holy Ghost,

21 Keep yourselves in the love of God, looking for the mercy of our Lord Jesus Christ unto eternal life.

22 And of some have compassion, making a difference:

Then there is one step left for us in our eternal walk with Jesus. That is the resurrection, which is the reuniting of our bodies and spirit forever. Scripture describes two resurrections. One being the first resurrection of the those who are righteous and the second of all the dead.

MATTHEW 27:52-54 KING JAMES VERSION (KJV)

52 And the graves were opened; and many bodies of the saints which slept arose,

53 And came out of the graves after his resurrection, and went into the holy city, and appeared unto many.

54 Now when the centurion, and they that were with him, watching Jesus, saw the earthquake, and those things that were done, they feared greatly, saying, Truly this was the Son of God.

LUKE 14:13-15 KING JAMES VERSION (KJV)

13 But when thou makest a feast, call the poor, the maimed, the lame, the blind:

14 And thou shalt be blessed; for they cannot recompense thee: for thou shalt be recompensed at the resurrection of the just.

15 And when one of them that sat at meat with him heard these things, he said unto him, Blessed is he that shall eat bread in the kingdom of God.

JOHN 5:28-30 KING JAMES VERSION (KJV)

28 Marvel not at this: for the hour is coming, in the which all that are in the graves shall hear his voice,

29 And shall come forth; they that have done good, unto the resurrection of life; and they that have done evil, unto the resurrection of damnation.

30 I can of mine own self do nothing: as I hear, I judge: and my judgment is just; because I seek not mine own will, but the will of the Father which hath sent me.

ROMANS 6:4-6 KING JAMES VERSION (KJV)

4 Therefore we are buried with him by baptism into death: that like as Christ was raised up from the dead by the glory of the Father, even so we also should walk in newness of life.

5 For if we have been planted together in the likeness of his death, we shall be also in the likeness of his resurrection:

6 Knowing this, that our old man is crucified with him, that the body of sin might be destroyed, that henceforth we should not serve sin.

1 CORINTHIANS 15:41-43 KING JAMES VERSION (KJV)

41 There is one glory of the sun, and another glory of the moon, and another glory of the stars: for one star differeth from another star in glory.

42 So also is the resurrection of the dead. It is sown in corruption; it is raised in incorruption:

43 It is sown in dishonour; it is raised in glory: it is sown in weakness; it is raised in power:

HEBREWS 6:1-3 AMPLIFIED BIBLE (AMP)

The Peril of Falling Away

1 Therefore let us get past the elementary stage in the teachings about the Christ, advancing on to maturity and perfection and spiritual completeness, [doing this] without laying again a foundation of repentance from dead works and of faith toward God,

2 of teaching about washings (ritual purifications), the laying on of hands, the resurrection of the dead, and eternal judgment. [These are all important matters in which you should have been proficient long ago.]

3 And we will do this [that is, proceed to maturity], if God permits.

Yes, it is time for us in the church to become mature in our faith and learn to walk with confidence in the promise of eternal life, filled with all the riches and happiness we need in our walk with God. We no longer need to wail and despair at a funeral, but instead we need to rejoice for one of our loved ones is in the hands of the Father and Son who will be just and fair in their treatment of them. We need to accept that the word of God is true and that we can trust what He says. I'll close with this testimony:

On a Labor Day weekend, several years ago, I received a call. My mother had died. They found her lying next to her bed and had called for an ambulance but, it didn't show up for about a half an hour and she could not be revived. My heart shrank in sorrow. Since we live in Tulsa, Oklahoma and she lived in St. Louis, I had to drive there. My wife went with me. On my way there while I was having the thoughts of grief and "why had this happened?" going through my mind, the quiet voice of the Lord said to me "This is not about death but the life she lived." All of a sudden, I was filled with a spirit of peace and comfort, knowing now that God was in control. He knew my anguish and loved me enough to bring a word of comfort and confirmation that He was in control so, I no longer needed to despair. I too have had to learn that He does not lie and there is more to life than the death of this body of ours.

JAMES 2:25-26 KING JAMES VERSION (KJV)

25 Likewise also was not Rahab the harlot justified by works, when she had received the messengers, and had sent them out another way?

26 For as the body without the spirit is dead, so faith without works is dead also.

EPHESIANS 2:11-13 AMPLIFIED BIBLE (AMP)

11 Therefore, remember that at one time you Gentiles by birth, who are called "Uncircumcision" by those who called themselves "Circumcision," [itself a mere mark] which is made in the flesh by human hands—

12 remember that at that time you were separated from Christ [excluded from any relationship with Him], alienated from the commonwealth of Israel, and strangers to the covenants of promise [with no share in the sacred Messianic promise and without knowledge of God's agreements], having no hope [in His promise] and [living] in the world without God.

13 But now [at this very moment] in Christ Jesus you who once were [so very] far away [from God] have been brought near [a]by the blood of Christ.

Footnotes:

Ephesians 2:13 Or in.

1 THESSALONIANS 4:12-18 KING JAMES VERSION (KJV)

12 That ye may walk honestly toward them that are without, and that ye may have lack of nothing.

13 But I would not have you to be ignorant, brethren, concerning them which are asleep, that ye sorrow not, even as others which have no hope.

14 For if we believe that Jesus died and rose again, even so them also which sleep in Jesus will God bring with him.

15 For this we say unto you by the word of the Lord, that we which are alive and remain unto the coming of the Lord shall not prevent them which are asleep.

16 For the Lord himself shall descend from heaven with a shout, with the voice of the archangel, and with the trump of God: and the dead in Christ shall rise first:

17 Then we which are alive and remain shall be caught up together with them in the clouds, to meet the Lord in the air: and so shall we ever be with the Lord.

18 Wherefore comfort one another with these words.

Eternal life and eternal existence differ. Scripture describes both. One is the state of living in bliss in God's presence the other is to be cast into outer darkness and living in eternal torment. As stated before, each depends on our choice to believe (accept Jesus as our Saviour) or not to believe. The condemnation of man is by his own choosing. All will have this choice either in this life or the one to come just as the souls in Paradise which died prior to His death and resurrection.

CHAPTER 2

How to Obtain Eternal Life

Eternal life is a gift. It cannot be obtained through worship of idols, potions, incantations, magic spells, preserving of your body, use of special devices or relics. No amount of money or influence can be used to obtain this nor fame, nor fortune nor even good deeds. Not even the evil spirits or the angles of the Satan can provide this. It is not a universal option afforded to everyone. We have become accustomed through media to seeing this all played out in various ways. We see vampires, zombies, demons, and other characters which supposedly can live on forever. Many have been indoctrinated into this realm through video games, games (the Ouija Board), literature, religions (voodoo, satanic cults, and even some Christian ministers) action figures, comic books, and other sources. No not even one we consider to be a "good person" can enter this just because of their good works or deeds. It is something that cannot be earned. Some have been taught that everyone will obtain eternal life but this is not verified by scripture. It is only their desire to try to make God and His desire for all men to repent as not necessary because God is good and loves us all and that Jesus died for all sin. Scripture clearly states that the only way to eternal life is through belief in Jesus the Christ and God the Father. Understand that belief not only carries with it the knowledge that God is real but it also involves repentance. Even the devil and his angles know that God is real but they have chosen not to repent or to not accept the authority of Jesus Christ or His ways.

JOHN 3:35-36 AMPLIFIED BIBLE (AMP)
35 The Father loves the Son and has given and entrusted all things into His hand.

³⁶ He who believes and trusts in the Son and accepts Him [as Savior] has eternal life [that is, already possesses it]; but he who does not believe the Son and chooses to reject Him, [disobeying Him and denying Him as Savior] will not see [eternal] life, but [instead] the wrath of God hangs over him continually."

According to scripture eternal life is only provided to those who believe on the one and only true God and Jesus the Christ of Nazareth. Yes, it does have provisions and conditions. Now you might say this is unfair because not everyone has had an opportunity to know or hear about God and Jesus. Well this as scripture explains, is not the case for all have had the opportunity to know God and all will have an opportunity to accept Jesus. So, let's delve into this. First let's look into what scripture says it takes to believe that God is real.

JOHN 5:23-25 KING JAMES VERSION (KJV)

²³ That all men should honour the Son, even as they honour the Father. He that honoureth not the Son honoureth not the Father which hath sent him.

²⁴ Verily, verily, I say unto you, He that heareth my word, and believeth on him that sent me, hath everlasting life, and shall not come into condemnation; but is passed from death unto life.

²⁵ Verily, verily, I say unto you, The hour is coming, and now is, when the dead shall hear the voice of the Son of God: and they that hear shall live.

ACTS 11:1-18 KING JAMES VERSION (KJV)

¹ And the apostles and brethren that were in Judaea heard that the Gentiles had also received the word of God.

² And when Peter was come up to Jerusalem, they that were of the circumcision contended with him,

³ Saying, Thou wentest in to men uncircumcised, and didst eat with them.

⁴ But Peter rehearsed the matter from the beginning, and expounded it by order unto them, saying,

⁵ I was in the city of Joppa praying: and in a trance I saw a vision, A certain vessel descend, as it had been a great sheet, let down from heaven by four corners; and it came even to me:

⁶ Upon the which when I had fastened mine eyes, I considered, and saw fourfooted beasts of the earth, and wild beasts, and creeping things, and fowls of the air.

⁷ And I heard a voice saying unto me, Arise, Peter; slay and eat.

⁸ But I said, Not so, Lord: for nothing common or unclean hath at any time entered into my mouth.

⁹ But the voice answered me again from heaven, What God hath cleansed, that call not thou common.

¹⁰ And this was done three times: and all were drawn up again into heaven.

¹¹ And, behold, immediately there were three men already come unto the house where I was, sent from Caesarea unto me.

¹² And the Spirit bade me go with them, nothing doubting. Moreover these six brethren accompanied me, and we entered into the man's house:

¹³ And he shewed us how he had seen an angel in his house, which stood and said unto him, Send men to Joppa, and call for Simon, whose surname is Peter;

¹⁴ Who shall tell thee words, whereby thou and all thy house shall be saved.

¹⁵ And as I began to speak, the Holy Ghost fell on them, as on us at the beginning.

¹⁶ Then remembered I the word of the Lord, how that he said, John indeed baptized with water; but ye shall be baptized with the Holy Ghost.

¹⁷ Forasmuch then as God gave them the like gift as he did unto us, who believed on the Lord Jesus Christ; what was I, that I could withstand God?

¹⁸ When they heard these things, they held their peace, and glorified God, saying, Then hath God also to the Gentiles granted repentance unto life.

ROMANS 2:6-8 AMPLIFIED BIBLE (AMP)

⁶ He will pay back to each person according to his deeds [justly, as his deeds deserve]:

⁷ to those who by persistence in doing good seek [unseen but certain heavenly] glory, honor, and immortality, [He will give the gift of] eternal life.

⁸ But for those who are selfishly ambitious and self-seeking and disobedient to the truth but responsive to wickedness, [there will be] wrath and indignation.

ROMANS 5:17-19 KING JAMES VERSION (KJV)

¹⁷ For if by one man's offence death reigned by one; much more they which receive abundance of grace and of the gift of righteousness shall reign in life by one, Jesus Christ.)

¹⁸ Therefore as by the offence of one judgment came upon all men to condemnation; even so by the righteousness of one the free gift came upon all men unto justification of life.

[19] *For as by one man's disobedience many were made sinners, so by the obedience of one shall many be made righteous.*

MATTHEW 19:16-22 KING JAMES VERSION (KJV)

[16] *And, behold, one came and said unto him, Good Master, what good thing shall I do, that I may have eternal life?*

[17] *And he said unto him, Why callest thou me good? there is none good but one, that is, God: but if thou wilt enter into life, keep the commandments.*

[18] *He saith unto him, Which? Jesus said, Thou shalt do no murder, Thou shalt not commit adultery, Thou shalt not steal, Thou shalt not bear false witness,*

[19] *Honour thy father and thy mother: and, Thou shalt love thy neighbour as thyself.*

[20] *The young man saith unto him, All these things have I kept from my youth up: what lack I yet?*

[21] *Jesus said unto him, If thou wilt be perfect, go and sell that thou hast, and give to the poor, and thou shalt have treasure in heaven: and come and follow me.*

[22] *But when the young man heard that saying, he went away sorrowful: for he had great possessions.*

ROMANS 3:26-28 AMPLIFIED BIBLE (AMP)

[26] *It was to demonstrate His righteousness at the present time, so that He would be just and the One who justifies those who have faith in Jesus [and rely confidently on Him as Savior].*

[27] *Then what becomes of [our] boasting? It is excluded [entirely ruled out, banished]. On what principle? On [the principle of good] works? No, but on the principle of faith.*

[28] *For we maintain that an individual is justified by faith distinctly apart from works of the Law [the observance of which has nothing to do with justification, that is, being declared free of the guilt of sin and made acceptable to God].*

I am led to point out there is a spirit realm which is intermingled with this life. So be aware that both function side by side. There are two parts to this realm. One is that of God and His righteous following and the other is Satan and his group of followers. The realm of God and His followers are a source of good while the realm of Satan and his followers are the source of all evil. Satan and his followers are opposed to God and their goal is to bring those who will follow them to the fate reserved for those who are evil.

ROMANS 1:15-32 KING JAMES VERSION (KJV)

[15] So, as much as in me is, I am ready to preach the gospel to you that are at Rome also.

[16] For I am not ashamed of the gospel of Christ: for it is the power of God unto salvation to every one that believeth; to the Jew first, and also to the Greek.

[17] For therein is the righteousness of God revealed from faith to faith: as it is written, The just shall live by faith.

[18] For the wrath of God is revealed from heaven against all ungodliness and unrighteousness of men, who hold the truth in unrighteousness;

[19] Because that which may be known of God is manifest in them; for God hath shewed it unto them.

[20] For the invisible things of him from the creation of the world are clearly seen, being understood by the things that are made, even his eternal power and Godhead; so that they are without excuse:

[21] Because that, when they knew God, they glorified him not as God, neither were thankful; but became vain in their imaginations, and their foolish heart was darkened.

[22] Professing themselves to be wise, they became fools,

[23] And changed the glory of the uncorruptible God into an image made like to corruptible man, and to birds, and fourfooted beasts, and creeping things.

[24] Wherefore God also gave them up to uncleanness through the lusts of their own hearts, to dishonour their own bodies between themselves:

[25] Who changed the truth of God into a lie, and worshipped and served the creature more than the Creator, who is blessed for ever. Amen.

[26] For this cause God gave them up unto vile affections: for even their women did change the natural use into that which is against nature:

[27] And likewise also the men, leaving the natural use of the woman, burned in their lust one toward another; men with men working that which is unseemly, and receiving in themselves that recompence of their error which was meet.

[28] And even as they did not like to retain God in their knowledge, God gave them over to a reprobate mind, to do those things which are not convenient;

[29] Being filled with all unrighteousness, fornication, wickedness, covetousness, maliciousness; full of envy, murder, debate, deceit, malignity; whisperers,

³⁰ Backbiters, haters of God, despiteful, proud, boasters, inventors of evil things, disobedient to parents,

³¹ Without understanding, covenantbreakers, without natural affection, implacable, unmerciful:

³² Who knowing the judgment of God, that they which commit such things are worthy of death, not only do the same, but have pleasure in them that do them.

ROMANS 1:15-32 AMPLIFIED BIBLE (AMP)

¹⁵ So, for my part, I am ready and eager to preach the gospel also to you who are in Rome.

¹⁶ I am not ashamed of the gospel, for it is the power of God for salvation [from His wrath and punishment] to everyone who believes [in Christ as Savior], to the Jew first and also to the Greek.

¹⁷ For in the gospel the righteousness of God is revealed, both springing from faith and leading to faith [disclosed in a way that awakens more faith]. As it is written and forever remains written, "The just and upright shall live by faith."

Unbelief and Its Consequences

¹⁸ For [God does not overlook sin and] the wrath of God is revealed from heaven against all ungodliness and unrighteousness of men who in their wickedness suppress and stifle the truth,

¹⁹ because that which is known about God is evident within them [in their inner consciousness], for God made it evident to them.

²⁰ For ever since the creation of the world His invisible attributes, His eternal power and divine nature, have been clearly seen, being understood through His workmanship [all His creation, the wonderful things that He has made], so that they [who fail to believe and trust in Him] are without excuse and without defense.

²¹ For even though [a]they knew God [as the Creator], they did not [b]honor Him as God or give thanks [for His wondrous creation]. On the contrary, they became worthless in their thinking [godless, with pointless reasonings, and silly speculations], and their foolish heart was darkened.

²² Claiming to be wise, they became fools,

²³ and exchanged the glory and majesty and excellence of the immortal God for [c]an image [worthless idols] in the shape of mortal man and birds and four-footed animals and reptiles.

²⁴ Therefore God gave them over in the lusts of their own hearts to [sexual] impurity, so that their bodies would be dishonored among them [abandoning them to the degrading power of sin],

²⁵ because [by choice] they exchanged the truth of God for a lie, and worshiped and served the creature rather than the Creator, who is blessed forever! Amen.

²⁶ For this reason God gave them over to degrading and vile passions; for their women exchanged the natural function for that which is unnatural [a function contrary to nature],

²⁷ and in the same way also the men turned away from the natural function of the woman and were consumed with their desire toward one another, men with men committing shameful acts and in return receiving in their own bodies the inevitable and appropriate penalty for their wrongdoing.

²⁸ And since they did not see fit to acknowledge God or consider Him worth knowing [as their Creator], God gave them over to a depraved mind, to do things which are improper and repulsive,

²⁹ until they were filled (permeated, saturated) with every kind of unrighteousness, wickedness, greed, evil; full of envy, murder, strife, deceit, malice and mean-spiritedness. They are gossips [spreading rumors],

³⁰ slanderers, haters of God, insolent, arrogant, boastful, inventors [of new forms] of evil, disobedient and disrespectful to parents,

³¹ without understanding, untrustworthy, unloving, unmerciful [without pity].

³² Although they know God's righteous decree and His judgment, that those who do such things deserve death, yet they not only do them, but they even [enthusiastically] approve and tolerate others who practice them.

Footnotes:

Romans 1:21 Anyone who attributes the existence of the world to chance or to a different creator is already guilty of deliberately rejecting God, because to deny the true God one must set aside common sense.

Romans 1:21 Lit glorify.

Romans 1:23 Paul's indictment of idolatry (images) is logical and devastating. He emphasizes that idols are essentially copies of living creatures, whether in human form (as, for example, in ancient Greek myth) or otherwise (as in Egyptian idolatry and metaphysics). These lifeless images are clearly powerless, and even the living creatures which they supposedly represent are either nonexistent hybrids and monsters, or else ordinary creatures on earth who could hardly create so much as a grain of sand.

The scriptures above talk about how God can be found if one really investigates the creation in which we live. Day after day, we are bombarded by so-called scientist trying their best to disprove the existence of God. They come up with theories which try to prove there is no intelligence behind the creation. Yet the evidence is to the contrary. Each part of the creation performs in predictable orderly behaviors. Many accept the theory of non-intelligent design because these are learned men and women who are well educated and who are preaching a doctrine or religion of happenstance and faith in nothing but man himself. If one carefully examines the results that they end up with, you will find that most of the time it is a restatement of what they set out to prove rather than a true representation of the facts. Each part of creation is proof of intelligent intent and design. Yes, the first book I was led to write is subtitled with a restatement of Einstein's theory ($E = M \times C^2$) which translates into energy is neither created nor destroyed. It is eternal in other words. If you look at the basic building block of all matter, both inanimate and animal, you find that there is a mysterious energy that holds them all together and the same atoms are the basis of them all. Yet learned men and women have tried to get us to believe this all occurred as a result of nothing out of nowhere. They start throwing common sense out the window in view of what we consider to be the wisdom of the day. So, which do you buy into, the faith of nothingness or into the faith of a creator? My vote is for the creator. Why are doctors able to come up with treatments for those who have specific problems if they have not found specific patterns which each of these follows? For me I see a creation that is ruled by order and intelligent design. I don't see a set of random acts. I am an engineer by training and what I have learned through science and math is that everything is governed by a set of rules which we use to make things that man can use in his daily life. What I see is a human body that has so many miraculous functions some of which are measurable and identifiable and some of which we unable to identify or can't understand, completely. We can see how they work such through intelligent thought and reasoning. Yes, even those who claim we can see how this came about by happenstance can't come up with an explanation for this or the fact that everything in the universe follows a set of rules by which they exist. Yes, just as the above scripture states, we follow made up, silly reasoning pretending to be wise and yet we are so foolish.

The rules of science are based on principles that we have found to be consistent. So why are we so intent on proving these wrong. These cannot be both right and wrong at the same time. Yes, these rules are imperfect but they provide a starting point which leads to improved rules. The more we learn, the better our understanding of these rules become. Intelligence is the basis of all consistency. Rules just don't establish themselves. They have a source. That source is God. We come up with theories which we can't prove. So, we make up results to support what we want the outcome to be. We replace the truth with a lie or just pure conjecture. We dismiss the dimension of the spirit because we are unable to put it into a test tube. Yet we keep searching for the missing link described by Darwin. We have had many who have claimed to do so and their results have proved false.

Summary

Eternal life requires faith in a God who is eternal and who wants to share this with his creation. The things required to obtain this are:

- Faith in God and His son Christ Jesus.
- A repentant life style.
- Accepting the proof of the true nature of God's creation and its intelligent design as proof of His existence.
- Accepting the instruction, He has provided in scripture.
- Being obedient to the transformational work of the Holy Spirit in our lives

That is why we are told in scripture to seek first the kingdom of God and his righteousness. We should have as goals in this life to:

- Learn to love the Lord our God with all our heart mind and strength.
- Allow the Holy Spirit to create in us a new heart so that we will love the Lord our God with all our heart mind and strength and to love our neighbors as ourselves.
- Allow the Holy Spirit to help transform us such that we will love living a righteous life style and to help us to learn to hate sin that we may become like Jesus being perfect as the Father in heaven is perfect.

If we make these our primary goals rather than what we consider to be our self-comfort then God's kingdom can easily be established. So, living a life style like Jesus is evidence we have eternal life. Remember that in scripture belief is more than just having knowledge of something. Belief means to not only accept or acknowledge but to do all that comes along with it which is where repentance begins. Scripture defines belief as a multiplicity of items not just acceptance. It so much more than that. It embodies repentance which is more than a onetime approach.

1 JOHN 3:1-3 KING JAMES VERSION

¹ Behold, what manner of love the Father hath bestowed upon us, that we should be called the sons of God: therefore the world knoweth us not, because it knew him not.

² Beloved, now are we the sons of God, and it doth not yet appear what we shall be: but we know that, when he shall appear, we shall be like him; for we shall see him as he is.

³ And every man that hath this hope in him purifieth himself, even as he is pure.

1 JOHN 1:8-9 KING JAMES VERSION (KJV)

⁸ If we say that we have no sin, we deceive ourselves, and the truth is not in us.

⁹ If we confess our sins, he is faithful and just to forgive us our sins, and to cleanse us from all unrighteousness.

1 JOHN 3:23-24 KING JAMES VERSION

²³ And this is his commandment, That we should believe on the name of his Son Jesus Christ, and love one another, as he gave us commandment.

²⁴ And he that keepeth his commandments dwelleth in him, and he in him. And hereby we know that he abideth in us, by the Spirit which he hath given us.

1 JOHN 5:1-3 KING JAMES VERSION

⁵ Whosoever believeth that Jesus is the Christ is born of God: and every one that loveth him that begat loveth him also that is begotten of him.

² By this we know that we love the children of God, when we love God, and keep his commandments.

³ For this is the love of God, that we keep his commandments: and his commandments are not grievous.

CHAPTER 3

There's Nothing Like the Real Thing

1 KINGS 17:15-23 KING JAMES VERSION

15 And she went and did according to the saying of Elijah: and she, and he, and her house, did eat many days.

16 And the barrel of meal wasted not, neither did the cruse of oil fail, according to the word of the Lord, which he spake by Elijah.

17 And it came to pass after these things, that the son of the woman, the mistress of the house, fell sick; and his sickness was so sore, that there was no breath left in him.

18 And she said unto Elijah, What have I to do with thee, O thou man of God? art thou come unto me to call my sin to remembrance, and to slay my son?

19 And he said unto her, Give me thy son. And he took him out of her bosom, and carried him up into a loft, where he abode, and laid him upon his own bed.

20 And he cried unto the Lord, and said, O Lord my God, hast thou also brought evil upon the widow with whom I sojourn, by slaying her son?

21 And he stretched himself upon the child three times, and cried unto the Lord, and said, O Lord my God, I pray thee, let this child's soul come into him again.

22 And the Lord heard the voice of Elijah; and the soul of the child came into him again, and he revived.

23 And Elijah took the child, and brought him down out of the chamber into the house, and delivered him unto his mother: and Elijah said, See, thy son liveth

JOHN 8:31-33 KING JAMES VERSION (KJV)

31 Then said Jesus to those Jews which believed on him, If ye continue in my word, then are ye my disciples indeed;
32 And ye shall know the truth, and the truth shall make you free.
33 They answered him, We be Abraham's seed, and were never in bondage to any man: how sayest thou, Ye shall be made free?

When the Spirit provided me the title for this chapter, He pointed me to a song title and to the training of Federal Agents. Now you might ask how these two relate to the scripture? Well here is what I was led to share. First of all, there was song from my early years which contained the words "there is nothing like the real thing baby". The song related to a relationship for what we considered true love. Now we know that this is what God is. He is true love. We are called to make a decision to love God with ultimate love and others the same way. In scripture we find where Jesus challenged John with this choice and had Him say it aloud so that he would recognize the depth of love Jesus was endowed with and wants us to see him the same way. Let's review this scripture.

JOHN 21:14-17 AMPLIFIED BIBLE (AMP)

14 This was now the third time that Jesus appeared to the disciples, after He had risen from the dead.
The Love Motivation
15 So when they had finished breakfast, Jesus said to Simon Peter, "Simon, son of John, do you love Me more than these [others do— with total commitment and devotion]?" He said to Him, "Yes, Lord; You know that I [a]love You [with a deep, personal affection, as for a close friend]." Jesus said to him, "Feed My lambs."
16 Again He said to him a second time, "Simon, son of John, do you love Me [with total commitment and devotion]?" He said to Him, "Yes, Lord; You know that I love You [with a deep, personal affection, as for a close friend]." Jesus said to him, "Shepherd My sheep."
17 He said to him the third time, "Simon, son of John, do you love Me [with a deep, personal affection for Me, as for a close friend]?" Peter was grieved that He asked him the third time, "Do you [really] [b]love Me [with a deep, personal affection, as for a close friend]?" And he said to Him, "Lord, You know everything; You know that I love You [with a deep, personal affection, as for a close friend]." Jesus said to him, "Feed My sheep.
Footnotes:

John 21:15 As indicated by the amplifications, Peter uses a different Greek word for love (phileo) than Jesus does (agapao) in His first two questions to Peter (see note v 17).
John 21:17 This time Jesus uses the same word for love that Peter previously used twice (phileo).

You might ask how this relates to eternal life. First you must understand God's reasoning behind providing us with eternal life. He provides us eternal life as a demonstration of how deeply He loves us as His own creation. To Him we are more than a passing thought or something He can discard. God provides us this because He created us from the very beginning out of His good pleasure, not out of necessity, nor for any other reason. He wanted to share His love and companionship with us. This is not a temporary situation but it relates to His appreciation and love for us. Therefore, He provided the opportunity for us to share the gift of eternal life if we so choose. Yes, as with all things in our relationship with God we have to accept Him, then He grants our entry into the eternal realm with Him. Now it doesn't mean that we will understand or know of our eternal state when He grants it. He has provided insight in His word for us to begin to know we have been accepted into this state with Him. That is one reason He has Jesus say in the Lord's Prayer "Thy will be done on earth as it in heaven". Heaven is an eternal realm. It has no end. So, God seeks to get us to know in various ways that He wants His creation to share the same state whether here on earth or in Heaven along with all that heaven represents. It is His desire that the same situation and conditions prevail in both places so that there is no difference between our existence in either place. Yes, eternity is as much about what heaven is about as well the other attributes which it represents.

Now let's go into how the Federal Agents fit into this picture. When the Spirit provided this title, I was lying in bed early in the morning. He brought to my memory a documentary I had seen on the training of Federal Agents. In this special it identified how the agents were trained to spot fake currency. It showed in order to spot fakes they were taught to know the real thing. They get to know each aspect, the feel of the paper and how to identify each detail no matter how minor. It is a matter of the touch and sight working together to know each and every little nuance included on the money. They study it over and over until they are comfortable and until it is embedded in their memory.

They were never shown any fakes but they were taught that if you know the real thing and identify its attributes you can spot a fake by what is what it should or shouldn't contain.

We can see the same principle in God's word. We can identify the fakes through the study of His word empowered by the Holy Spirit. Without the Holy Spirit we can be easily led astray in our interpretation of His word and its true intent. Case in point we see this in Christ's challenge from the devil when He had finished His forty day fast. The devil quoted scripture as it was written (without understanding) and applied a distorted meaning in an attempt to hide its real intent, just as he did with Eve in the garden. Many use scripture to support their wishes and not apply it in the way God intended.

Jesus knew the real thing, so He could not be confused or misled by the wrong interpretation of God's word. As I have been led over and over again in the works which I have been led to write, we need the Holy Spirit guiding us each time we read scripture. Through the Holy Spirit we learn the touch feel and every nuance of the gospel just as the federal agents are guided in their learning process to know the real thing. When we do study under the guidance of the Holy Spirit, we can learn to spot the counterfeit because we know the real thing. The Holy Spirt is necessary because He was the truth of each passage and wants to teach it to us.

At this point I am led to share something from someone else's testimony. He stated that he had avoided the Christian religion for many years. This was because he heard so many different interpretations of scripture that he did not know what to believe. Yes, he had been confused by Christian preachers. Each one provided his own interpretation of the same gospel and each was different and they didn't agree. All he heard was contradicting interpretations of God's word. It was only when he was introduced to the true love of God and the Holy Spirit, by the work of our Chattanooga congregation, that He was opened to the call of following Christ Jesus. Yes, all he had heard was the counterfeit by man's wisdom and did not understand the truth because He had not known the real or true gospel. So even when he heard the real, he was not willing to except it until the Holy Spirit helped him understand it. Many churches misuse scripture today to gain power, money, popularity in the eyes of men, or for promoting immoral behavior, lusts of the flesh or as a tool of the devil to promote all manner of iniquity. Many try to use their intellect to interpret scripture and that just doesn't work. One day, in spite of all of this, this gentleman had had his confusion cleared up. Here is a quote of a portion of what he shared in his own words.

PRAYER IS WORKING FOR MY BOY & ME..by Randall[2]

I've never been a church going person nor a guy who prays. I guess always believed in God but never did give much attention to God. I didn't even own a bible till a few days ago. Praying was only something religious people did! And they cannot even agree on the bible. I hated school but at least you could trust what was being taught there. I mean 2 plus 2 equals 4 and nobody argues it. When it comes to God, everyone wants to be an expert on religion, but nobody can agree on even simple items of religion.

Why trust what they are teaching when their own kind cannot agree on what the bible saying. It is more important to most religious church going people to be smarter than the other church goer about God, than it is to help those who need to get close to God. I wonder if they understand their efforts to be smarter about God than the other church down the street makes it harder for those outside these churches to trust God. I saw a story at the library claiming Chattanooga spends 9 times more money on teaching people religion stuff than solving the homeless crisis. Just don't think this was what Jesus had in mind when he was on the cross. Maybe I am too sensitive as my 6-year-old son and I are sleeping in my truck and eating at the community kitchen. Never wanted to be homeless but we are. When my girlfriend (mother of my son) split with me, she made sure her brother fired me from my job of 9 years. My son lost his mom, his home, his security in like 45 seconds when we were ordered by police to leave the house or I could go to jail with my boy going into the system. A guy I met at the kitchen told me about his church and said it was crazy because it loves crazy people. He convinced me they could help get my son into school. I went to church with him.

First time in 19 years I went to church. My son loves it. He wants to go every day. I am in church 2 times a week. Here is my witness. They gave me a bible showing me how to read it in a way it is easy to connect with God. They gave us simple things to talk to God

---

[2] This testimony was copied by permission of the Chattanooga Community of Christ Crumb Bucket newsletter Editor

about. I had only been doing this for a week when my miracle began showing up.

See just as this gentleman we hear too much which is false that we march to the tune of the wrong beat. We battle each other with one-upmanship. We are constantly trying to outdo each other so the end result is just what is stated in this man's testimony. Case in point, we hear very often that we should pray for what we want or name it and claim it and God will answer that prayer. The problem is that God will only answer a prayer that is in line with His will and plans. If we don't know these, we will ask for a lot and not receive what we ask for in the way we wanted. He will not support wrong in any form. So, we need to learn what the real thing is (what is His will). Even if we believe the meaning is clear to us, we need to ask Him how this applies to His true purposes. That way we come to know the real thing. It is best to be careful and find out first what His perfect will is because sometimes we don't have a clear understanding of everything. If we only pray thy will be done. What good is it if we don't come to know what His will is. We don't need to continue asking the wrong things. He wants us to mature in our knowledge of Him. That takes study with prayer and fasting. Note that fasting without prayer leads to frustration. Life can be frustrating when we don't get what we feel we deserve. While listening to a sermon the other day, I heard this being expressed. We become discouraged, angry and disappointed when we don't get what we feel we deserve as a result of our efforts. We expect complimentary results when we are good. (A pat on the back in return for good works and punishment in return for evil.) Just as Job's expectation were related in scripture when all the world seemed to be unjustly caving in on him. We expect to receive rewards based on how we live our lives. We expect good outcomes in return for what we consider good conduct. Our motivation should be to do all things in love for God and our fellow saints, even if it comes to enduring hardships.

- When we do what we see as right we expect the same in return. Just as Job did.
- When we do wrong, we want to escape the punishment or least to have it minimized.
- Job felt he had always done the right thing so He did not deserve bad treatment. He felt he was righteous and so no ill would come his way.

- Then, there are those things we consider to be unexplainable. Those things which occur for reasons we don't feel we deserve. Much the same as Job experienced.
- Just as Job, who do we blame, God? Why not? Isn't He in control of all things?

JOB 32:1-3 AMPLIFIED BIBLE (AMP)

Elihu Rebukes Job

¹ So these three men ceased answering Job, because he was righteous in his own eyes [and could not be persuaded otherwise by them].

² But Elihu the son of Barachel the Buzite, of the family of Ram, became indignant. His indignation was kindled and burned and he became upset with Job because he justified himself rather than God [and even expressed doubts about God's character].

³ Elihu's anger burned against Job's three friends because they had found no answer [and were unable to determine Job's error], and yet they had condemned Job and declared him to be in the wrong [and responsible for his own afflictions].

Just as Job, when we are hurting, all we care about is relief. Without the power of Godly love in us can't seem to see past the suffering. Our only concern is and our main focus is getting rid of our pain and suffering. Nothing or anyone else seems to matter. We are very selfish at this point. Without the Holy Spirit providing His peace through God's love implanted in us we suffer anguish. We have heard this quoted so much "Yeah though I walk the valley of the shadow of death I will fear no evil". Man, in his own will cannot follow this path or live up to this scripture. Most of us recognize this from the 23rd Psalm. It is only when we shift our focus from ourselves to others can this can occur. Scripture says pray for those who spitefully use you or pray that God will see you through this situation that He might be glorified. Yes, the real thing is God's love and His promise of eternal life embedded in us which provides us strength to face anything. Yes, the real thing is even though we are in God's arms we still will have trouble in this world. Let's review Jesus' council to His disciples.

JOHN 16:32-33 KING JAMES VERSION (KJV)

³² Behold, the hour cometh, yea, is now come, that ye shall be scattered, every man to his own, and shall leave me alone: and yet I am not alone, because the Father is with me.

³³ These things I have spoken unto you, that in me ye might have peace. In the world ye shall have tribulation: but be of good cheer; I have overcome the world.

He does not promise, as many people state, that following Him will be a bed of roses. According to Jesus, we face a road scattered with troubles which we must be prepared to face head on. Yes, we hear the confused interpretation of scripture which has caused many to go astray. He does not try to fool you into thinking by following Him life will be easy. What He does say is it will be easier with Him than without Him. He doesn't say we won't have enemies or that we will never have to face sickness or disease or come to financial ruin. What he does say is He will be by our side and support us through trials and tribulations. As a matter of fact, He tells us just as He was hated and mistreated those who follow Him will be treated the same.

Summary

I am led to bring Ephesian 2 to your attention. The above is summed up in this scripture.

EPHESIANS 2 KING JAMES VERSION (KJV)

¹ And you hath he quickened, who were dead in trespasses and sins;
² Wherein in time past ye walked according to the course of this world, according to the prince of the power of the air, the spirit that now worketh in the children of disobedience:
³ Among whom also we all had our conversation in times past in the lusts of our flesh, fulfilling the desires of the flesh and of the mind; and were by nature the children of wrath, even as others.
⁴ But God, who is rich in mercy, for his great love wherewith he loved us,
⁵ Even when we were dead in sins, hath quickened us together with Christ, (by grace ye are saved;)
⁶ And hath raised us up together, and made us sit together in heavenly places in Christ Jesus:
⁷ That in the ages to come he might shew the exceeding riches of his grace in his kindness toward us through Christ Jesus.
⁸ For by grace are ye saved through faith; and that not of yourselves: it is the gift of God:
⁹ Not of works, lest any man should boast.

[10] *For we are his workmanship, created in Christ Jesus unto good works, which God hath before ordained that we should walk in them.*

[11] *Wherefore remember, that ye being in time past Gentiles in the flesh, who are called Uncircumcision by that which is called the Circumcision in the flesh made by hands;*

[12] *That at that time ye were without Christ, being aliens from the commonwealth of Israel, and strangers from the covenants of promise, having no hope, and without God in the world:*

[13] *But now in Christ Jesus ye who sometimes were far off are made nigh by the blood of Christ.*

[14] *For he is our peace, who hath made both one, and hath broken down the middle wall of partition between us;*

[15] *Having abolished in his flesh the enmity, even the law of commandments contained in ordinances; for to make in himself of twain one new man, so making peace;*

[16] *And that he might reconcile both unto God in one body by the cross, having slain the enmity thereby:*

[17] *And came and preached peace to you which were afar off, and to them that were nigh.*

[18] *For through him we both have access by one Spirit unto the Father.*

[19] *Now therefore ye are no more strangers and foreigners, but fellow citizens with the saints, and of the household of God;*

[20] *And are built upon the foundation of the apostles and prophets, Jesus Christ himself being the chief corner stone;*

[21] *In whom all the building fitly framed together groweth unto an holy temple in the Lord:*

[22] *In whom ye also are builded together for an habitation of God through the Spirit.*

Here we see the truth of God's work to redeem men to Himself. Yes, it is stated in many places.

- We are saved by God's grace because He loves us.
- Jesus is the source of all that we are and all that we are to become after we accept them (repent)
- God has always had a plan for the salvation of man. It is His grace not man's efforts that accomplish this.
- We are raised from sin that we might learn good works and do them.

- When we entered into a covenant with Him, we were granted life eternal or habitation with Him in heavenly places.

As we begin our eternal life walk, we are to choose to be led by the work of the Holy Spirit to do the good works. Examples of which may be found in the scripture which God has provided. God originally created us to do good works. Since we know this, we should be seeking to allow the transforming work of the Holy Spirit in us by always seeking His guidance that we may be the workmanship that God ordained from the beginning. This should be a priority every day of our life. We should always be seeking to first establish the kingdom of God (His love in us and trust in Him) in all that we do that it may be here on earth as it is in heaven.

EPHESIANS 2:9-11 KING JAMES VERSION (KJV)

9 Not of works, lest any man should boast.

10 For we are his workmanship, created in Christ Jesus unto good works, which God hath before ordained that we should walk in them.

11 Wherefore remember, that ye being in time past Gentiles in the flesh, who are called Uncircumcision by that which is called the Circumcision in the flesh made by hands;

COLOSSIANS 3:9-11 KING JAMES VERSION (KJV)

9 Lie not one to another, seeing that ye have put off the old man with his deeds;

10 And have put on the new man, which is renewed in knowledge after the image of him that created him:

11 Where there is neither Greek nor Jew, circumcision nor uncircumcision, Barbarian, Scythian, bond nor free: but Christ is all, and in all.

This cannot be emphasized enough, "seek ye first the kingdom of God and His righteousness". We are told then you shall know the truth and the truth will set you free. The truth lies in Christ Jesus and the Holy Spirit and a people converted to be as Jesus is. Jesus demonstrated this by the life He lived while on earth. You and I can do it. So, our choice is Eternal life with God (life of forgiveness and regeneration by God and Christ Jesus) or eternal damnation (life without God tormented by our sins, the choice to reject God and His ways).

CHAPTER 4

When Does Eternal Life Start and End?

According to scripture eternal life begins for when we believe on the Lord Jesus Christ and God the Father who sent Him. Now in scripture we find believing is more than an intellectual exercise. It carries more than just acknowledging or just having the knowledge that something is. It includes an acceptance of them and their precepts or set of requirements. This means that we have not only received the knowledge of their existence but we also accept that they have ideals (precepts, conditions, parameters and so on) to which we must conform. We are literally agreeing to accept God and Jesus and the Holy Spirit along with the provisions they have established. We are receiving forgiveness along with our commitment to follow Jesus and His commandments. Let's start exploring this.

First, I am led to point out that we have an example provided for us in scripture of someone knowing Jesus and God and also knowing what they stand for and what they ask of us. We are told the devil and his angels know Jesus and God but rejected them. Here are a few scriptural references.

MARK 1:33-34 AMPLIFIED BIBLE (AMP)
³³ until the whole city had gathered together at the door.
³⁴ And Jesus healed many who were suffering with various diseases; and He drove out many demons, but would not allow the demons to speak, because they knew Him [recognizing Him as the Son of God].

MARK 5:1-17 KING JAMES VERSION (KJV)

¹ And they came over unto the other side of the sea, into the country of the Gadarenes.

² And when he was come out of the ship, immediately there met him out of the tombs a man with an unclean spirit,

³ Who had his dwelling among the tombs; and no man could bind him, no, not with chains:

⁴ Because that he had been often bound with fetters and chains, and the chains had been plucked asunder by him, and the fetters broken in pieces: neither could any man tame him.

⁵ And always, night and day, he was in the mountains, and in the tombs, crying, and cutting himself with stones.

⁶ But when he saw Jesus afar off, he ran and worshipped him,

⁷ And cried with a loud voice, and said, What have I to do with thee, Jesus, thou Son of the most high God? I adjure thee by God, that thou torment me not.

⁸ For he said unto him, Come out of the man, thou unclean spirit.

⁹ And he asked him, What is thy name? And he answered, saying, My name is Legion: for we are many.

¹⁰ And he besought him much that he would not send them away out of the country.

¹¹ Now there was there nigh unto the mountains a great herd of swine feeding.

¹² And all the devils besought him, saying, Send us into the swine, that we may enter into them.

¹³ And forthwith Jesus gave them leave. And the unclean spirits went out, and entered into the swine: and the herd ran violently down a steep place into the sea, (they were about two thousand;) and were choked in the sea.

LUKE 4:32-34 AMPLIFIED BIBLE (AMP)

³² and they were surprised [almost overwhelmed] at His teaching, because His message was [given] with authority and power and great ability.

³³ There was a man in the synagogue who was possessed by the spirit of an unclean demon; and he cried out with a loud and terrible voice,

³⁴ "Let us alone! [a]What business do we have [in common] with each other, Jesus of Nazareth? Have You come to destroy us? I know who You are—the Holy One of God!"

Footnotes:

Luke 4:34 Lit What to me and to you; cf note Matt 8:29.

MATTHEW 8:29 AMPLIFIED BIBLE (AMP)

[29] And they screamed out, "[a]What business do we have [in common] with each other, Son of God? Have You come to torment us before the appointed time [of judgment]?"

Footnotes:

Matthew 8:29 Lit What to us and to you, originally a Hebrew idiom which does not translate well into English. The idiom is meant to bluntly inform the other person that the speaker is not aware of any obligation between them, and does not wish to deal with the other person (cf 2 Sam 16:10). It can also express the speaker's protest that he has not harmed the other individual, and therefore should not suffer harm at the hands of that person (cf 1 Kin 17:18).

As can be readily seen from the above scriptures the devils or demons all have a knowledge of Jesus and His authority over them. They also have a knowledge of the steps they need to take to really know Him and follow Him but they refused to do so long ago. You can see how they respectfully approach Him and know what their fate is. They understand that Jesus is the Son of God and they know and accept that because of their rejection of His ways they are consigned to go into a state of punishment at an appointed time. They know they have committed the unpardonable sin. It is also referred to as denying the Holy Ghost. Those who have come to a full knowledge of Him and reject Him afterward can no longer be granted forgiveness of sin in this world nor in the world to come. Now consider this scripture.

EZEKIEL 28:11-19 KING JAMES VERSION (KJV)

[11] Moreover the word of the Lord came unto me, saying,

[12] Son of man, take up a lamentation upon the king of Tyrus, and say unto him, Thus saith the Lord God; Thou sealest up the sum, full of wisdom, and perfect in beauty.

[13] Thou hast been in Eden the garden of God; every precious stone was thy covering, the sardius, topaz, and the diamond, the beryl, the onyx, and the jasper, the sapphire, the emerald, and the carbuncle, and gold: the workmanship of thy tabrets and of thy pipes was prepared in thee in the day that thou wast created.

[14] Thou art the anointed cherub that covereth; and I have set thee so: thou wast upon the holy mountain of God; thou hast walked up and down in the midst of the stones of fire.

[15] Thou wast perfect in thy ways from the day that thou wast created, till iniquity was found in thee.

[16] By the multitude of thy merchandise they have filled the midst of thee with violence, and thou hast sinned: therefore I will cast thee

as profane out of the mountain of God: and I will destroy thee, O covering cherub, from the midst of the stones of fire.

17 Thine heart was lifted up because of thy beauty, thou hast corrupted thy wisdom by reason of thy brightness: I will cast thee to the ground, I will lay thee before kings, that they may behold thee.

18 Thou hast defiled thy sanctuaries by the multitude of thine iniquities, by the iniquity of thy traffick; therefore will I bring forth a fire from the midst of thee, it shall devour thee, and I will bring thee to ashes upon the earth in the sight of all them that behold thee.

19 All they that know thee among the people shall be astonished at thee: thou shalt be a terror, and never shalt thou be any more.

I am led to provide a brief description of what the unpardonable sin is. This is because so many believe they have committed this act but really have yet to do so. First, you must have an in-depth knowledge of who Jesus Christ and God are and have an in-depth understanding of their precepts and conditions completely. After this you had been offered an opportunity to repent but rejected it. Then there is no more opportunity after that to receive forgiveness. Yes, there are those who have been back sliding once they were baptized (been practicing the sins they were involved in prior to baptism) but they have not completely rejected that God is the one and only true God and Jesus Christ is his son. Until one has had an opportunity to do this such as the Angels in heaven which followed Lucifer out of heaven then you have not committed the unpardonable sin. This is as simple as I am able to relate this to you now. I'll discuss this more in my next book on Revelation part 1. Read this scripture again.

EZEKIEL 28:11-19 KING JAMES VERSION (KJV)

11 Moreover the word of the Lord came unto me, saying,

12 Son of man, take up a lamentation upon the king of Tyrus, and say unto him, Thus saith the Lord God; Thou sealest up the sum, full of wisdom, and perfect in beauty.

13 Thou hast been in Eden the garden of God; every precious stone was thy covering, the sardius, topaz, and the diamond, the beryl, the onyx, and the jasper, the sapphire, the emerald, and the carbuncle, and gold: the workmanship of thy tabrets and of thy pipes was prepared in thee in the day that thou wast created.

14 Thou art the anointed cherub that covereth; and I have set thee so: thou wast upon the holy mountain of God; thou hast walked up and down in the midst of the stones of fire.

15 Thou wast perfect in thy ways from the day that thou wast created, till iniquity was found in thee.

16 By the multitude of thy merchandise they have filled the midst of thee with violence, and thou hast sinned: therefore I will cast thee as profane out of the mountain of God: and I will destroy thee, O covering cherub, from the midst of the stones of fire.

17 Thine heart was lifted up because of thy beauty, thou hast corrupted thy wisdom by reason of thy brightness: I will cast thee to the ground, I will lay thee before kings, that they may behold thee.

18 Thou hast defiled thy sanctuaries by the multitude of thine iniquities, by the iniquity of thy traffick; therefore will I bring forth a fire from the midst of thee, it shall devour thee, and I will bring thee to ashes upon the earth in the sight of all them that behold thee.

19 All they that know thee among the people shall be astonished at thee: thou shalt be a terror, and never shalt thou be any more.

REVELATION 12:1-9 KING JAMES VERSION (KJV)

1 And there appeared a great wonder in heaven; a woman clothed with the sun, and the moon under her feet, and upon her head a crown of twelve stars:

2 And she being with child cried, travailing in birth, and pained to be delivered.

3 And there appeared another wonder in heaven; and behold a great red dragon, having seven heads and ten horns, and seven crowns upon his heads.

4 And his tail drew the third part of the stars of heaven, and did cast them to the earth: and the dragon stood before the woman which was ready to be delivered, for to devour her child as soon as it was born.

5 And she brought forth a man child, who was to rule all nations with a rod of iron: and her child was caught up unto God, and to his throne.

6 And the woman fled into the wilderness, where she hath a place prepared of God, that they should feed her there a thousand two hundred and threescore days.

7 And there was war in heaven: Michael and his angels fought against the dragon; and the dragon fought and his angels,

⁸ And prevailed not; neither was their place found any more in heaven.
⁹ And the great dragon was cast out, that old serpent, called the Devil, and Satan, which deceiveth the whole world: he was cast out into the earth, and his angels were cast out with him.

Summary

Here we can see that believing is more than knowing the identity of God and Jesus Christ, but it requires repentance and a life style lived in accordance with the attributes of the righteousness of God. We who have accepted Christ as savior gained eternal life when we believed and evidence this each day by our choice to follow Him in doing good works and exhibiting the righteousness of God empowered by the Holy Spirit which was provided at our baptism and to some even before. When we believe, in every since of the term, eternity was granted to us that very day. So, life eternal is something those who believe and are living on this earth today have. It began the moment we first believed. It is not universally provided to all men or angels as some profess. Those who profess this are distorting the gospel and do not know or speak the truth. There is a difference between eternal life and eternal existence. Here are a few scriptures to demonstrate this.

1 TIMOTHY 1:15-17 KING JAMES VERSION (KJV)
¹⁵ This is a faithful saying, and worthy of all acceptation, that Christ Jesus came into the world to save sinners; of whom I am chief.
¹⁶ Howbeit for this cause I obtained mercy, that in me first Jesus Christ might shew forth all longsuffering, for a pattern to them which should hereafter believe on him to life everlasting.
¹⁷ Now unto the King eternal, immortal, invisible, the only wise God, be honour and glory for ever and ever. Amen.

GENESIS 15:1-7 KING JAMES VERSION (KJV)
¹ After these things the word of the Lord came unto Abram in a vision, saying, Fear not, Abram: I am thy shield, and thy exceeding great reward.
² And Abram said, Lord God, what wilt thou give me, seeing I go childless, and the steward of my house is this Eliezer of Damascus?
³ And Abram said, Behold, to me thou hast given no seed: and, lo, one born in my house is mine heir.

⁴ And, behold, the word of the Lord came unto him, saying, This shall not be thine heir; but he that shall come forth out of thine own bowels shall be thine heir.

⁵ And he brought him forth abroad, and said, Look now toward heaven, and tell the stars, if thou be able to number them: and he said unto him, So shall thy seed be.

⁶ And he believed in the Lord; and he counted it to him for righteousness.

⁷ And he said unto him, I am the Lord that brought thee out of Ur of the Chaldees, to give thee this land to inherit it.

EXODUS 4:30-31 KING JAMES VERSION (KJV)

³⁰ And Aaron spake all the words which the Lord had spoken unto Moses, and did the signs in the sight of the people.

³¹ And the people believed: and when they heard that the Lord had visited the children of Israel, and that he had looked upon their affliction, then they bowed their heads and worshipped.

PSALM 78:21-23 KING JAMES VERSION (KJV)

²¹ Therefore the Lord heard this, and was wroth: so a fire was kindled against Jacob, and anger also came up against Israel;

²² Because they believed not in God, and trusted not in his salvation:

²³ Though he had commanded the clouds from above, and opened the doors of heaven,

JONAH 3:1-10 KING JAMES VERSION (KJV)

¹ And the word of the Lord came unto Jonah the second time, saying,

² Arise, go unto Nineveh, that great city, and preach unto it the preaching that I bid thee.

³ So Jonah arose, and went unto Nineveh, according to the word of the Lord. Now Nineveh was an exceeding great city of three days' journey.

⁴ And Jonah began to enter into the city a day's journey, and he cried, and said, Yet forty days, and Nineveh shall be overthrown.

⁵ So the people of Nineveh believed God, and proclaimed a fast, and put on sackcloth, from the greatest of them even to the least of them.

⁶ For word came unto the king of Nineveh, and he arose from his throne, and he laid his robe from him, and covered him with sackcloth, and sat in ashes.

⁷ And he caused it to be proclaimed and published through Nineveh by the decree of the king and his nobles, saying, Let neither man nor beast, herd nor flock, taste any thing: let them not feed, nor drink water:

[8] *But let man and beast be covered with sackcloth, and cry mightily unto God: yea, let them turn every one from his evil way, and from the violence that is in their hands.*

[9] *Who can tell if God will turn and repent, and turn away from his fierce anger, that we perish not?*

[10] *And God saw their works, that they turned from their evil way; and God repented of the evil, that he had said that he would do unto them; and he did it not.*

CHAPTER 5

What are the Conditions for Eternal Life?

According to the scripture it starts when a person has repented and accepted the one true God and Jesus His son. It sounds simple yet the complexity comes in the fact that most don't know of or accept that this has happened. They see the end of this body's term on earth as the start of eternal life. Even though scripture describes this as beginning here on earth we just don't seem to grasp it or understand this is the case. Yes, we quote scripture and sing songs but we just don't understand that we started our eternal existence when we accepted Christ Jesus. To us life on this earth is the most precious thing we have so anything else is just wishful thinking. That is why we are so afraid of dying or in the case of those who commit suicide as a way to escape the troubles of this world.

The conditions then for eternal life come down to two items. One is the fact that we accept Jesus and Father God as creator and the source of all living. Then we have accepted that the Holy Spirit is to work in us to remake us into the image of Christ Jesus. Two is our realization that this process has already started so that we are to allow the Holy Spirit to be our daily guide so that the will of God will be done here on earth as it is in heaven. Now this is a gift of God to us.

The degree to which we comply with this gift determines how God supplies us with the place which we fit in His heavenly kingdom. Yes, the degree with which we find comfort here on earth is the degree with which we will have comfort with in our heavenly existence. That is why scripture states the same state or mind we have here on earth will be the same state with which we will face God with when we stand before Him when our spirit leaves this body. He then allots a spot in heaven which fits the degree of acceptance of His guidance with which we have had here on earth. Scripture describes this as the glories.

2 TIMOTHY 1:8-9 KING JAMES VERSION (KJV)

8 Be not thou therefore ashamed of the testimony of our Lord, nor of me his prisoner: but be thou partaker of the afflictions of the gospel according to the power of God;

9 Who hath saved us, and called us with an holy calling, not according to our works, but according to his own purpose and grace, which was given us in Christ Jesus before the world began,

1 CORINTHIANS 15:40-42 KING JAMES VERSION (KJV)

40 There are also celestial bodies, and bodies terrestrial: but the glory of the celestial is one, and the glory of the terrestrial is another.

41 There is one glory of the sun, and another glory of the moon, and another glory of the stars: for one star differeth from another star in glory.

42 So also is the resurrection of the dead. It is sown in corruption; it is raised in incorruption:

The conditions for our eternal existence are simple. Yet we are to allow the change in our attitudes so that we choose the ways of God rather than the ways of man. So, one condition is our understanding that our ways just as we are unacceptable to God. Let's see how scripture states it.

1. All have sinned and have come short of the glory of God.

ROMANS 3:22-24 KING JAMES VERSION (KJV)

22 Even the righteousness of God which is by faith of Jesus Christ unto all and upon all them that believe: for there is no difference:

23 For all have sinned, and come short of the glory of God;

24 Being justified freely by his grace through the redemption that is in Christ Jesus:

2. Sin is a bitter root which has to be cast out of our lives. We cannot do this in an appropriate way so we must allow God to do it.

HEBREWS 12:14-25 AMPLIFIED BIBLE (AMP)

14 Continually pursue peace with everyone, and the sanctification without which no one will [ever] see the Lord.

15 See to it that no one falls short of God's grace; that no root of resentment springs up and causes trouble, and by it many be defiled;

16 and [see to it] that no one is immoral or godless like Esau, who sold his own birthright for a single meal.

17 For you know that later on, when he wanted [to regain title to] his inheritance of the blessing, he was rejected, for he found no opportunity for repentance [there was no way to repair what he had done, no chance to recall the choice he had made], even though he sought for it with [bitter] tears.

Contrast of Sinai and Zion

18 For you have not come [as did the Israelites in the wilderness] to a mountain that can be touched and to a blazing fire, and to gloom and darkness and a raging windstorm,

19 and to the blast of a trumpet and a sound of words [such that] those who heard it begged that nothing more be said to them.

20 For they could not bear the command, "If even a wild animal touches the mountain, it will be stoned [to death]."

21 In fact, so terrifying was the sight, that Moses said, "I am filled with fear and trembling."

22 But you have come to Mount Zion and to the city of the living God, the heavenly Jerusalem, and to myriads of angels [in festive gathering],

23 and to the general assembly and assembly of the firstborn who are registered [as citizens] in heaven, and to God, who is Judge of all, and to the spirits of the righteous (the redeemed in heaven) who have been made perfect [bringing them to their final glory],

24 and to Jesus, the Mediator of a new covenant [uniting God and man], and to the sprinkled blood, which speaks [of mercy], a better and nobler and more gracious message than the blood of Abel [which cried out for vengeance].

The Unshaken Kingdom

25 See to it that you do not refuse [to listen to] Him who is speaking [to you now]. For if those [sons of Israel] did not escape when they refused [to listen to] him who warned them on earth [revealing God's will], how much less will we escape if we turn our backs on Him who warns from heaven?

3. We need to come to the point where we hate sin. We must recognize the devastating impact that it has on us as well as others.

PSALM 36:1-3 AMPLIFIED BIBLE (AMP)

Wickedness of Men and Lovingkindness of God.
To the Chief Musician. A Psalm of David the servant of the Lord.
[1] *Transgression speaks [like an oracle] to the wicked (godless) [deep] within his heart; There is no fear (dread) of God before his eyes.*
[2] *For he flatters and deceives himself in his own eyes Thinking that his sinfulness will not be discovered and hated [by God].*
[3] *The words of his mouth are wicked and deceitful; He has ceased to be wise and to do good.*

JOHN 3:19-21 AMPLIFIED BIBLE (AMP)

[19] *This is the judgment [that is, the cause for indictment, the test by which people are judged, the basis for the sentence]: the Light has come into the world, and people loved the [a]darkness rather than the Light, for their deeds were evil.*
[20] *For every wrongdoer hates the Light, and does not come to the Light [but shrinks from it] for fear that his [sinful, worthless] activities will be exposed and condemned.*
[21] *But whoever practices truth [and does what is right—morally, ethically, spiritually] comes to the Light, so that his works may be plainly shown to be what they are—accomplished in God [divinely prompted, done with God's help, in dependence on Him]."*
Footnotes:
John 3:19 See note 1:5.

JOHN 1:5 AMPLIFIED BIBLE

[5] *The Light shines on in the [a]darkness, and the darkness did not understand it or overpower it or appropriate it or absorb it [and is unreceptive to it].*
Footnotes
John 1:5 I.e. the world immersed in sin: all that stands in opposition to God and biblical truth.

4. We must allow the Holy Spirit to work within us to clean sin from our minds and replace it with God's righteousness. This is the process in scripture which is termed renewing our minds. It is a willingness on our part to allow God to replace our sinful ways with His righteous ways.

MATTHEW 6:30-34 KING JAMES VERSION

[30] *Wherefore, if God so clothe the grass of the field, which to day is, and to morrow is cast into the oven, shall he not much more clothe you, O ye of little faith?*

31 Therefore take no thought, saying, What shall we eat? or, What shall we drink? or, Wherewithal shall we be clothed?

32 (For after all these things do the Gentiles seek:) for your heavenly Father knoweth that ye have need of all these things.

33 But seek ye first the kingdom of God, and his righteousness; and all these things shall be added unto you.

34 Take therefore no thought for the morrow: for the morrow shall take thought for the things of itself. Sufficient unto the day is the evil thereof.

2 SAMUEL 23:1-5 KING JAMES VERSION

1 Now these be the last words of David. David the son of Jesse said, and the man who was raised up on high, the anointed of the God of Jacob, and the sweet psalmist of Israel, said,

2 The Spirit of the Lord spake by me, and his word was in my tongue.

3 The God of Israel said, the Rock of Israel spake to me, He that ruleth over men must be just, ruling in the fear of God.

4 And he shall be as the light of the morning, when the sun riseth, even a morning without clouds; as the tender grass springing out of the earth by clear shining after rain.

5 Although my house be not so with God; yet he hath made with me an everlasting covenant, ordered in all things, and sure: for this is all my salvation, and all my desire, although he make it not to grow.

Here we can see that King David understood that he had been granted salvation through the rock of Israel and that he and his family had not done as instructed.

5.   It should become to us as God told Israel. Our existence is to be an example to the world that following God and doing His will is something that is desirable and the benefits that it brings.

MATTHEW 5:15-17 KING JAMES VERSION (KJV)

15 Neither do men light a candle, and put it under a bushel, but on a candlestick; and it giveth light unto all that are in the house.

16 Let your light so shine before men, that they may see your good works, and glorify your Father which is in heaven.

17 Think not that I am come to destroy the law, or the prophets: I am not come to destroy, but to fulfil.

6.   It is more than going to church or spouting scripture. We become a living breathing example of scripture here and now.

The point is we are to do things differently. We are to be in this world but not a product of it. Rather than living to keep up with the Jones' we are to allow the Holy Spirit to change us into the spitting image of Christ here so that we show forth God's glory to all.

Summary

Jesus offers the gift of Eternal life to all who believe on Him. Yet it carries with it some prerequisites which are evidence of what it takes to receive this gift. Yes, belief constitutes more than just recognizing Jesus as our Lord and savior. In it is incorporated so many other things. It is not just one meaning which we allot to it. Consider this below.

1.   One major condition included is that a person must repent.

JOHN 3:16-22 KING JAMES VERSION (KJV)

[16] For God so loved the world, that he gave his only begotten Son, that whosoever believeth in him should not perish, but have everlasting life.

[17] For God sent not his Son into the world to condemn the world; but that the world through him might be saved.

[18] He that believeth on him is not condemned: but he that believeth not is condemned already, because he hath not believed in the name of the only begotten Son of God.

[19] And this is the condemnation, that light is come into the world, and men loved darkness rather than light, because their deeds were evil.

[20] For every one that doeth evil hateth the light, neither cometh to the light, lest his deeds should be reproved.

[21] But he that doeth truth cometh to the light, that his deeds may be made manifest, that they are wrought in God.

[22] After these things came Jesus and his disciples into the land of Judaea; and there he tarried with them, and baptized.

   a.   This includes accepting that God deserves to be glorified and accepting that all have sinned and come short of the glory of God. So, we agree to accept God which includes trusting what He says do.

REVELATION 16:8-10 KING JAMES VERSION (KJV)

[8] And the fourth angel poured out his vial upon the sun; and power was given unto him to scorch men with fire.

[9] And men were scorched with great heat, and blasphemed the name of God, which hath power over these plagues: and they repented not to give him glory.

[10] And the fifth angel poured out his vial upon the seat of the beast; and his kingdom was full of darkness; and they gnawed their tongues for pain,

ROMANS 15:5-7 KING JAMES VERSION (KJV)

5 Now the God of patience and consolation grant you to be likeminded one toward another according to Christ Jesus:

6 That ye may with one mind and one mouth glorify God, even the Father of our Lord Jesus Christ.

7 Wherefore receive ye one another, as Christ also received us to the glory of God.

    b. We must confess our fleshly sin and be willing to cooperate with God so that He can remove these inclinations from within us.

ACTS 19:17-19 AMPLIFIED BIBLE

17 This became known to all who lived in Ephesus, both Jews and Greeks. And fear fell upon them all, and the name of the Lord Jesus was magnified and exalted.

18 Many of those who had become believers were coming, confessing and disclosing their [former sinful] practices.

19 And many of those who had practiced magical arts collected their books and [throwing book after book on the pile] began burning them in front of everyone. They calculated their value and found it to be [a]50,000 pieces of silver.

Footnotes

Acts 19:19 Each piece, possibly a drachma, may have been about a day's wage.

We are called to walk in the Holy Spirit, which means following what He teaches us and allowing Him to repair the scars incurred in our lives and cooperating with Him so we can be released from those sinful lusts within us. This all comes down to Him implanting God's love for the Godhead, ourselves and others within us.

One day as I was awakening from sleep the Lord started sharing with me some things which I had done which were controlling me in the wrong way and I needed to repent from these to allow Him to change these into something righteous. As an example, I made a vow to myself that when I got older, I would eat as many snickers bars as I could whenever I wanted. Though this may seem as a childish whim. It became one of those things imbedded in my psyche which I now have a predisposition to follow as an adult. Another along the same lines was the vow I made to drink soda pop whenever and as much as I wanted when I was older and out of my parent's influence. You see we all have these types of oaths embedded within us and though the ones pointed out may seem minor they loom very large in the life of a diabetic. Just as He has shown these things to me, He will reveal to you those things in you which are not pleasing to Him and which are not beneficial to you and His kingdom. We are also encumbered with so many temptations which we must not give into. Many are tempted to commit adultery or to steal yet with the help of the Spirit we can overcome performing these tendencies. According to scripture all men are to be tempted but Jesus added in the Lord's prayer that we ask to not to be led into temptation and for us to delivered from evil.

EPHESIANS 4:20-29 KING JAMES VERSION

20 But ye have not so learned Christ;

21 If so be that ye have heard him, and have been taught by him, as the truth is in Jesus:

22 That ye put off concerning the former conversation the old man, which is corrupt according to the deceitful lusts;

23 And be renewed in the spirit of your mind;

24 And that ye put on the new man, which after God is created in righteousness and true holiness.

25 Wherefore putting away lying, speak every man truth with his neighbour: for we are members one of another.

26 Be ye angry, and sin not: let not the sun go down upon your wrath:

27 Neither give place to the devil.

28 Let him that stole steal no more: but rather let him labour, working with his hands the thing which is good, that he may have to give to him that needeth.

29 Let no corrupt communication proceed out of your mouth, but that which is good to the use of edifying, that it may minister grace unto the hearers.

We can't allow anything such as these to keep us from allowing God to renew our minds and to allow Him to purge the sin from our minds so that He can replace it with righteous thinking and doing. Yes, we have many such things of even greater prominence which we don't readily recall which separates us from doing things the way God intended in the beginning. For we can't do this by ourselves for all we can do is make a greater mess of our lives. We can go to a psychiatrist, but He will only try to get us to can control these obsessions. Whereas God wants to help us to be set completely free from these. At best, psychiatrist are only about 30% successful. That's why God has told us to come as we are but to not to stay as we are. Many only heed the part about coming as you are and don't understand there is a more important step which must be taken. That is to not stay in our sinful state. He makes a promise to put a new heart and mind within us replacing our heart of stone with one like that of Jesus. A Heart which lives to only do those things pleasing to the Father, in love. Jesus stated that if we know Him and the things which He did while on this earth, then we will know the Father. So, following the things which Jesus did will qualify as following what the Father does.

JOHN 5:18-20 KING JAMES VERSION

18 Therefore the Jews sought the more to kill him, because he not only had broken the sabbath, but said also that God was his Father, making himself equal with God.

19 Then answered Jesus and said unto them, Verily, verily, I say unto you, The Son can do nothing of himself, but what he seeth the Father do: for what things soever he doeth, these also doeth the Son likewise.

20 For the Father loveth the Son, and sheweth him all things that himself doeth: and he will shew him greater works than these, that ye may marvel.

CHAPTER 6

Eternal Life Is for Whom

Who can receive eternal life? We all start this life on a level playing field. We are all provided a conscience with a pre-programed set of instructions of what is right and wrong. It is not based on the multitude of items we have or the lack of them. This is a gift God provides for each one of us. This is a built-in moral code (the conscience) that is provided so we can use to guide us to live a life for God or we can ignore it and we can choose to follow our own lusts or the way of the devices of the devil. Now let's consider God's attitude toward man. In scripture God's viewpoint toward man is described in several scripture references. Let's look into a few of these.

GENESIS 1:26-28 KING JAMES VERSION

26 And God said, Let us make man in our image, after our likeness: and let them have dominion over the fish of the sea, and over the fowl of the air, and over the cattle, and over all the earth, and over every creeping thing that creepeth upon the earth.

27 So God created man in his own image, in the image of God created he him; male and female created he them.

28 And God blessed them, and God said unto them, Be fruitful, and multiply, and replenish the earth, and subdue it: and have dominion over the fish of the sea, and over the fowl of the air, and over every living thing that moveth upon the earth.

LUKE 12:31-33 KING JAMES VERSION

31 But rather seek ye the kingdom of God; and all these things shall be added unto you.

32 Fear not, little flock; for it is your Father's good pleasure to give you the kingdom.

³³ Sell that ye have, and give alms; provide yourselves bags which wax not old, a treasure in the heavens that faileth not, where no thief approacheth, neither moth corrupteth.

EPHESIANS 1:8-10 KING JAMES VERSION

⁸ Wherein he hath abounded toward us in all wisdom and prudence;

⁹ Having made known unto us the mystery of his will, according to his good pleasure which he hath purposed in himself:

¹⁰ That in the dispensation of the fulness of times he might gather together in one all things in Christ, both which are in heaven, and which are on earth; even in him:

PHILIPPIANS 2:12-14 KING JAMES VERSION

¹² Wherefore, my beloved, as ye have always obeyed, not as in my presence only, but now much more in my absence, work out your own salvation with fear and trembling.

¹³ For it is God which worketh in you both to will and to do of his good pleasure.

¹⁴ Do all things without murmurings and disputings:

2 PETER 3:1-16 KING JAMES VERSION

¹ This second epistle, beloved, I now write unto you; in both which I stir up your pure minds by way of remembrance:

² That ye may be mindful of the words which were spoken before by the holy prophets, and of the commandment of us the apostles of the Lord and Saviour:

³ Knowing this first, that there shall come in the last days scoffers, walking after their own lusts,

⁴ And saying, Where is the promise of his coming? for since the fathers fell asleep, all things continue as they were from the beginning of the creation.

⁵ For this they willingly are ignorant of, that by the word of God the heavens were of old, and the earth standing out of the water and in the water:

⁶ Whereby the world that then was, being overflowed with water, perished:

⁷ But the heavens and the earth, which are now, by the same word are kept in store, reserved unto fire against the day of judgment and perdition of ungodly men.

⁸ But, beloved, be not ignorant of this one thing, that one day is with the Lord as a thousand years, and a thousand years as one day.

⁹ The Lord is not slack concerning his promise, as some men count slackness; but is longsuffering to us-ward, not willing that any should perish, but that all should come to repentance.

¹⁰ But the day of the Lord will come as a thief in the night; in the which the heavens shall pass away with a great noise, and the elements shall melt with fervent heat, the earth also and the works that are therein shall be burned up.
¹¹ Seeing then that all these things shall be dissolved, what manner of persons ought ye to be in all holy conversation and godliness,
¹² Looking for and hasting unto the coming of the day of God, wherein the heavens being on fire shall be dissolved, and the elements shall melt with fervent heat?
¹³ Nevertheless we, according to his promise, look for new heavens and a new earth, wherein dwelleth righteousness.
¹⁴ Wherefore, beloved, seeing that ye look for such things, be diligent that ye may be found of him in peace, without spot, and blameless.
¹⁵ And account that the longsuffering of our Lord is salvation; even as our beloved brother Paul also according to the wisdom given unto him hath written unto you;
¹⁶ As also in all his epistles, speaking in them of these things; in which are some things hard to be understood, which they that are unlearned and unstable wrest, as they do also the other scriptures, unto their own destruction.

In the beginning man was created in the image and likeness of God. So, man was created to be like God. Not to be God but to match or to mirror His character and form. Man was created out of God's good pleasure. It was not a whim or just a passing thought. It has pleased God to do this so that it was nothing that He did out of remorse or spite. Man is a special part of His creation. Unlike a tree or a rock man was endowed with special attributes which other parts of the creation were not. So, the intent behind man's creation was for Him to do good things in accordance with the design of God. Yet God loved us enough to allow us to be able to choose to do or not to do His good pleasure. He gave us the free will to choose to serve or not serve Him. His desire is for all to be saved. Yet He allows us to choose to either accept or reject salvation. Even though we are a chosen part of His creation, we are free to choose, as it states in John 3:16-21, not to serve Him which results in self condemnation. We have had the opportunity to choose life. Yet we make a choice of what comes as result of our unwillingness to be rejuvenated in His likeness and to follow His will. In spite of our choices to live against His will, He provides a provision for us to be redeemed from our fallen state. He is patient with us and He allots us the opportunity to accept Him providing us with all the time we need to do this. He equipped us with a conscience programmed with right guidance. He provided us with creativity and intelligence to be able to perceive Him by His creation. It is He who draws us to repent but He will not force us to do so.

1 TIMOTHY 2:1-6 KING JAMES VERSION

[1] *I exhort therefore, that, first of all, supplications, prayers, intercessions, and giving of thanks, be made for all men;*

[2] *For kings, and for all that are in authority; that we may lead a quiet and peaceable life in all godliness and honesty.*

[3] *For this is good and acceptable in the sight of God our Saviour;*

[4] *Who will have all men to be saved, and to come unto the knowledge of the truth.*

[5] *For there is one God, and one mediator between God and men, the man Christ Jesus;*

[6] *Who gave himself a ransom for all, to be testified in due time.*

JOHN 3:16-21 KING JAMES VERSION

[16] *For God so loved the world, that he gave his only begotten Son, that whosoever believeth in him should not perish, but have everlasting life.*

[17] *For God sent not his Son into the world to condemn the world; but that the world through him might be saved.*

[18] *He that believeth on him is not condemned: but he that believeth not is condemned already, because he hath not believed in the name of the only begotten Son of God.*

[19] *And this is the condemnation, that light is come into the world, and men loved darkness rather than light, because their deeds were evil.*

[20] *For every one that doeth evil hateth the light, neither cometh to the light, lest his deeds should be reproved.*

[21] *But he that doeth truth cometh to the light, that his deeds may be made manifest, that they are wrought in God.*

REVELATION 21:5-7 KING JAMES VERSION

[5] *And he that sat upon the throne said, Behold, I make all things new. And he said unto me, Write: for these words are true and faithful.*

[6] *And he said unto me, It is done. I am Alpha and Omega, the beginning and the end. I will give unto him that is athirst of the fountain of the water of life freely.*

⁷ He that overcometh shall inherit all things; and I will be his God, and he shall be my son.
REVELATION 22:16-18 KING JAMES VERSION
¹⁶ I Jesus have sent mine angel to testify unto you these things in the churches. I am the root and the offspring of David, and the bright and morning star.
¹⁷ And the Spirit and the bride say, Come. And let him that heareth say, Come. And let him that is athirst come. And whosoever will, let him take the water of life freely.
¹⁸ For I testify unto every man that heareth the words of the prophecy of this book, If any man shall add unto these things, God shall add unto him the plagues that are written in this book:

The invitation is provided to all through the sacrifice of Jesus to receive God's pardon for our choices and to allow Him to redo our sinful life style and turn it into a life style as He originally intended. That is why we can't clean up ourselves because it is His good pleasure to bring to pass remaking us in His image with His righteous ways. All that we do on our own would be flawed. God's desire has always been for none of His creation to perish but for all of it to rest in His presence. The pattern He desired is exemplified when scripture describes how He approached Adam in the garden. He also gave man the opportunity at mount Sinai but they refused. He continues to communicate to those who are willing to listen and who will accept His voice. We were created to share His presence and share freely because God has provided all that is necessary for life both physical and spiritual. He gave Adam authority to name all the animals and He directly told Adam what was and what was not acceptable but He left the choice up to Adam. When Adam decided to follow Eve's invitation which went against God's directives, then and only then, was he separated from God's presence and the ability to grasp the tree of eternal life.

God has always allotted us the opportunity to either accept or reject His ways and direction.

Summary

The gift of eternal life is open to all but only those who are written the Lamb's book of life will receive it. You might say how do we go about being included in this book. It was established from the very beginning based on God's foreknowledge of whether you would accept or reject Him and how we choose to accept the instructions provided in our conscience.

PSALM 69:20-29 KING JAMES VERSION (KJV)

[20] *Reproach hath broken my heart; and I am full of heaviness: and I looked for some to take pity, but there was none; and for comforters, but I found none.*

[21] *They gave me also gall for my meat; and in my thirst they gave me vinegar to drink.*

[22] *Let their table become a snare before them: and that which should have been for their welfare, let it become a trap.*

[23] *Let their eyes be darkened, that they see not; and make their loins continually to shake.*

[24] *Pour out thine indignation upon them, and let thy wrathful anger take hold of them.*

[25] *Let their habitation be desolate; and let none dwell in their tents.*

[26] *For they persecute him whom thou hast smitten; and they talk to the grief of those whom thou hast wounded.*

[27] *Add iniquity unto their iniquity: and let them not come into thy righteousness.*

[28] *Let them be blotted out of the book of the living, and not be written with the righteous.*

[29] *But I am poor and sorrowful: let thy salvation, O God, set me up on high.*

PHILIPPIANS 4:2-4 NEW INTERNATIONAL VERSION (NIV)

[2] *I plead with Euodia and I plead with Syntyche to be of the same mind in the Lord.*

[3] *Yes, and I ask you, my true companion, help these women since they have contended at my side in the cause of the gospel, along with Clement and the rest of my co-workers, whose names are in the book of life.*

Final Exhortations

[4] *Rejoice in the Lord always. I will say it again: Rejoice!*

REVELATION 13:7-9 NEW INTERNATIONAL VERSION (NIV)

[7] *It was given power to wage war against God's holy people and to conquer them. And it was given authority over every tribe, people, language and nation.*

[8] *All inhabitants of the earth will worship the beast—all whose names have not been written in the Lamb's book of life, the Lamb who was slain from the creation of the world.[a]*

[9] *Whoever has ears, let them hear.*

Footnotes:

Revelation 13:8 Or written from the creation of the world in the book of life belonging to the Lamb who was slain

Some claim this is predestination but it is not so. For we all have the ability to make the choice to serve Him here on this earth in this life or in the period beyond. Yes, God can amend this book as needed. You see we all have a recorder within us. It is our conscience. This is to be what God uses as a final statement or judgement of the guilt or innocence of each person.

REVELATION 3:4-6 KING JAMES VERSION (KJV)

⁴ Thou hast a few names even in Sardis which have not defiled their garments; and they shall walk with me in white: for they are worthy.

⁵ He that overcometh, the same shall be clothed in white raiment; and I will not blot out his name out of the book of life, but I will confess his name before my Father, and before his angels.

⁶ He that hath an ear, let him hear what the Spirit saith unto the churches.

REVELATION 20:11-13 KING JAMES VERSION (KJV)

¹¹ And I saw a great white throne, and him that sat on it, from whose face the earth and the heaven fled away; and there was found no place for them.

¹² And I saw the dead, small and great, stand before God; and the books were opened: and another book was opened, which is the book of life: and the dead were judged out of those things which were written in the books, according to their works.

¹³ And the sea gave up the dead which were in it; and death and hell delivered up the dead which were in them: and they were judged every man according to their works.

ACTS 24:15-16 AMPLIFIED BIBLE (AMP)

¹⁵ having [the same] hope in God which these men cherish themselves, that there shall certainly be a resurrection of [the dead], both of the righteous and of the wicked.

¹⁶ In view of this, I also do my best and strive always to have a clear conscience before God and before men.

ROMANS 2:14-16 KING JAMES VERSION (KJV)

¹⁴ For when the Gentiles, which have not the law, do by nature the things contained in the law, these, having not the law, are a law unto themselves:

¹⁵ Which shew the work of the law written in their hearts, their conscience also bearing witness, and their thoughts the mean while accusing or else excusing one another;)

[16] *In the day when God shall judge the secrets of men by Jesus Christ according to my gospel*

2 CORINTHIANS 1:11-13 AMPLIFIED BIBLE (AMP)

[11] *while you join in helping us by your prayers. Then thanks will be given by many persons on our behalf for the gracious gift [of deliverance] granted to us through the prayers of many [believers]. Paul's Integrity*

[12] *This is our [reason for] proud confidence: our conscience testifies that we have conducted ourselves in the world [in general], and especially toward you, with pure motives and godly sincerity, not in human wisdom, but in the grace of God [that is, His gracious lovingkindness that leads people to Christ and spiritual maturity].*

[13] *For we write you nothing other than what you read and understand [there is no double meaning in what we say]. And I hope you will [accurately] understand [divine things] until the end;*

1 TIMOTHY 1:18-20 AMPLIFIED BIBLE (AMP)

[18] *This command I entrust to you, Timothy, my son, in accordance with the prophecies previously made concerning you, so that [inspired and aided] by them you may fight the good fight [in contending with false teachers],*

[19] *keeping your faith [leaning completely on God with absolute trust and confidence in His guidance] and having a good conscience; for some [people] have rejected [their moral compass] and have made a shipwreck of their faith.*

[20] *Among these are Hymenaeus and Alexander, whom I have [a]handed over to Satan, so that they will be disciplined and taught not to blaspheme.*

Footnotes:

1 Timothy 1:20 I.e. expelled from the safety of the church

TITUS 1:14-16 KING JAMES VERSION (KJV)

[14] *Not giving heed to Jewish fables, and commandments of men, that turn from the truth.*

[15] *Unto the pure all things are pure: but unto them that are defiled and unbelieving is nothing pure; but even their mind and conscience is defiled.*

[16] *They profess that they know God; but in works they deny him, being abominable, and disobedient, and unto every good work reprobate.*

REVELATION 20:11-13 AMPLIFIED BIBLE (AMP)

The Final Judgment

[11] *And I saw a great white throne and Him who was seated upon it, from whose presence earth and heaven fled away, and no place*

was found for them [for this heaven and earth are passing away].
¹² And I saw the dead, the great and the small, standing before the throne, and books were opened. Then another book was opened, which is the Book of Life; and the dead were judged according to what they had done as written in the books [that is, everything done while on earth].
¹³ And the sea gave up the dead who were in it, and death and Hades (the realm of the dead) surrendered the dead who were in them; and they were judged and sentenced, every one according to their deeds.

As Jesus states, He did not come to condemn man but man has condemned himself because man has refused to accept Jesus as His savour from and for our sinful acts. All will have an opportunity to do this either in this world or the world to come. This was demonstrated in the description of how Jesus went and taught the souls in paradise during the three-day period between His death and resurrection.

Just as the apostles of old, we are reluctant to accept the resurrection as fact. Jesus is constantly working to prove this to those who are willing to accept the truth. It is detailed in scripture how they all deserted when He was sent to the cross. It was only after Jesus visited on several occasions when they accepted His being resurrected. Many today see this as not plausible but we will all see Jesus face to face either in this world or the one to come. You see we all can come to the knowledge of His existence by observing His creation or we can be like some who want to claim all is happenstance or mysteriously just appeared from nothing. Many say there is no god because of circumstances or life events but they omit the fact that there is an evil presence which works to perform acts which leads us to disbelieve in the God of creation. So, as it states in scripture choose this day whom you will serve but as for me and my house, I choose the Lord.

JOSHUA 24:14-16 KING JAMES VERSION

¹⁴ Now therefore fear the Lord, and serve him in sincerity and in truth: and put away the gods which your fathers served on the other side of the flood, and in Egypt; and serve ye the Lord.
¹⁵ And if it seem evil unto you to serve the Lord, choose you this day whom ye will serve; whether the gods which your fathers served that were on the other side of the flood, or the gods of the Amorites, in whose land ye dwell: but as for me and my house, we will serve the Lord.

16 And the people answered and said, God forbid that we should forsake the Lord, to serve other gods;

One more point to share. Eternal life differs from living forever. As scripture states it is a life where we share the comfort of God's presence. While others will be excluded from this. In the scripture it describes both --- those living in bliss with God (eternal life) --- and those living in torment with their sin (eternal torment). We all will live in eternally in one state or another, bliss or torment.

LUKE 16:19-31 AMPLIFIED BIBLE (AMP)

The Rich Man and Lazarus

19 "Now there was a certain rich man who was habitually dressed in expensive purple and fine linen, and celebrated and lived joyously in splendor every day.

20 And a poor man named Lazarus, was laid at his gate, covered with sores.

21 He [eagerly] longed to eat the crumbs which fell from the rich man's table. Besides, even the dogs were coming and licking his sores.

22 Now it happened that the poor man died and his spirit was carried away by the angels to Abraham's [a]bosom (paradise); and the rich man also died and was buried.

23 In Hades (the realm of the dead), being in torment, he looked up and saw Abraham far away and Lazarus in his bosom (paradise). 24 And he cried out, 'Father Abraham, have mercy on me, and send Lazarus so that he may dip the tip of his finger in water and cool my tongue, because I am in severe agony in this flame.'

25 But Abraham said, 'Son, remember that in your lifetime you received your good things [all the comforts and delights], and Lazarus likewise bad things [all the discomforts and distresses]; but now he is comforted here [in paradise], while you are in severe agony.

26 And besides all this, between us and you [people] a great chasm has been fixed, so that those who want to come over from here to you will not be able, and none may cross over from there to us.'

27 So the rich man said, 'Then, father [Abraham], I beg you to send Lazarus to my father's house—

28 for I have five brothers—in order that he may solemnly warn them and witness to them, so that they too will not come to this place of torment.'

29 But Abraham said, 'They have [the Scriptures given by] Moses and the [writings of the] Prophets; let them listen to them.'

[30] He replied, 'No, father Abraham, but if someone from the dead goes to them, they will repent [they will change their old way of thinking and seek God and His righteousness].'

[31] And he said to him, 'If they do not listen to [the messages of] Moses and the Prophets, they will not be persuaded even if someone rises from the dead.'"

Footnotes:

Luke 16:22 Or lap. The Greek word basically means a fold, and could refer either to the fold of a robe over the chest or to the fold of a lap, formed when the legs are placed together. In either case, being "in Abraham's bosom" (v 23) is an image reflecting a blissful place of comfort and security.

LUKE 16:19-31 KING JAMES VERSION (KJV)

[19] There was a certain rich man, which was clothed in purple and fine linen, and fared sumptuously every day:

[20] And there was a certain beggar named Lazarus, which was laid at his gate, full of sores,

[21] And desiring to be fed with the crumbs which fell from the rich man's table: moreover the dogs came and licked his sores.

[22] And it came to pass, that the beggar died, and was carried by the angels into Abraham's bosom: the rich man also died, and was buried;

[23] And in hell he lift up his eyes, being in torments, and seeth Abraham afar off, and Lazarus in his bosom.

[24] And he cried and said, Father Abraham, have mercy on me, and send Lazarus, that he may dip the tip of his finger in water, and cool my tongue; for I am tormented in this flame.

[25] But Abraham said, Son, remember that thou in thy lifetime receivedst thy good things, and likewise Lazarus evil things: but now he is comforted, and thou art tormented.

[26] And beside all this, between us and you there is a great gulf fixed: so that they which would pass from hence to you cannot; neither can they pass to us, that would come from thence.

[27] Then he said, I pray thee therefore, father, that thou wouldest send him to my father's house:

[28] For I have five brethren; that he may testify unto them, lest they also come into this place of torment.

[29] Abraham saith unto him, They have Moses and the prophets; let them hear them.

[30] And he said, Nay, father Abraham: but if one went unto them from the dead, they will repent.

31 And he said unto him, If they hear not Moses and the prophets, neither will they be persuaded, though one rose from the dead.

LUKE 23:38-44 AMPLIFIED BIBLE (AMP)

38 Now there was also an inscription above Him: "THIS IS THE KING OF THE JEWS."

39 One of the criminals who had been hanged [on a cross beside Him] kept hurling abuse at Him, saying, "Are You not the Christ? Save Yourself and us [from death]!"

40 But the other one rebuked him, saying, "Do you not even fear God, since you are under the same sentence of condemnation?

41 We are suffering justly, because we are getting what we deserve for what we have done; but this Man has done nothing wrong."

42 And he was saying, "Jesus, [please] remember me when You come into Your kingdom!"

43 Jesus said to him, "I assure you and most solemnly say to you, today you will be with Me in [a]Paradise."

44 It was now about the sixth hour (noon), and darkness came over the whole land until the ninth hour (3:00 p.m.),

Footnotes:

Luke 23:43 I.e. possibly the third heaven, the special place or "garden" (Gen 2:8-10) between death and resurrection.

2 PETER 2:3-22 AMPLIFIED BIBLE (AMP)

3 And in their greed they will exploit you with false arguments and twisted doctrine. Their sentence [of condemnation which God has decreed] from a time long ago is not idle [but is still in force], and their destruction and deepening misery is not asleep [but is on its way].

4 [a]For if God did not [even] spare angels that sinned, but threw them into [b]hell and sent them to pits of gloom to be kept [there] for judgment;

5 and if He did not spare the ancient world, but protected Noah, a preacher of righteousness, with seven others, when He brought [the judgment of] a flood upon the world of the ungodly;

6 and if He condemned the cities of Sodom and Gomorrah to destruction by reducing them to ashes, having made them an example to those who would live ungodly lives thereafter;

7 and if He rescued righteous [c]Lot, who was tormented by the immoral conduct of unprincipled and ungodly men

8 (for that just man, while living among them, felt his righteous soul tormented day after day by what he saw and heard of their lawless acts),

⁹ then [in light of the fact that all this is true, be sure that] the Lord knows how to rescue the godly from trial, and how to keep the unrighteous under punishment until the day of judgment,

¹⁰ and especially [d]those who indulge in the corrupt passions of the sin nature, and despise authority. Presumptuous and reckless, self-willed and arrogant [creatures, despising the majesty of the Lord], they do not tremble when they revile angelic majesties,

¹¹ whereas even angels who are superior in might and power do not bring a reviling (defaming) accusation against them before the Lord.

¹² But these [false teachers], like unreasoning animals, [mere] creatures of instinct, born to be captured and destroyed, reviling things they do not understand, will also perish in their own corruption [in their destroying they will be destroyed],

¹³ suffering wrong [destined for punishment] as the wages of doing wrong. They count it a delight to revel in the daytime [living luxuriously]. They are stains and blemishes [on mankind], reveling in their [e]deceptions even as they feast with you.

¹⁴ They have eyes full of adultery, constantly looking for sin, enticing and luring away unstable souls. Having hearts trained in greed, [they are] children of a curse.

¹⁵ Abandoning the straight road [that is, the right way to live], they have gone astray; they have followed the way of [the false teacher] Balaam the son of Beor, who loved the reward of wickedness;

¹⁶ but he was rebuked for his own transgression: a mute donkey spoke with a man's voice and restrained the prophet's madness.

¹⁷ These [false teachers] are springs without water and mists driven by a tempest, for whom is reserved the gloom of black darkness.

¹⁸ For uttering arrogant words of vanity [pompous words disguised to sound scholarly or profound, but meaning nothing and containing no spiritual truth], they beguile and lure using lustful desires, by sensuality, those who barely escape from the ones who live in error.

¹⁹ They promise them liberty, when they themselves are the slaves of depravity—for by whatever anyone is defeated and overcome, to that [person, thing, philosophy, or concept] he is continually enslaved.

²⁰ For if, after they have escaped the pollutions of the world by [personal] knowledge of our Lord and Savior Jesus Christ, they are again entangled in them and are overcome, their last condition has become worse for them than the first.

[21] *For it would have been better for them not to have [personally] known the way of righteousness, than to have known it and then to have turned back from the holy commandment [verbally] handed on to them.*

[22] *The thing spoken of in the true proverb has happened to them, "The dog returns to his own vomit," and, "A sow is washed only to wallow [again] in the mire."*

Footnotes:

2 Peter 2:4 This verse begins one of the longest sentences in the NT. The sentence concludes in v 10a.

2 Peter 2:4 For emphasis Peter uses a word (tartarus) from Greek mythology describing a hell reserved for the most horrendous of people to emphasize the terrible doom awaiting false prophets and teachers who manipulate and twist the truth of the gospel message.

2 Peter 2:7 Lot was the nephew of Abraham and the son of Haran. He traveled with his uncle to Canaan and eventually settled in Sodom because of its proximity to good grazing land for his flocks. Peter presents a side of Lot not easily inferred from the OT account.

2 Peter 2:10 In the descriptions that follow, Peter may specifically have in mind the false teachers of whom he spoke in vv 1-3.

2 Peter 2:13 One early ms reads love feasts.

REVELATION 2:6-8 AMPLIFIED BIBLE (AMP)

[6] *Yet you have this [to your credit], that you hate the works and corrupt teachings of the [a]Nicolaitans [that mislead and delude the people], which I also hate.*

[7] *He who has an ear, let him hear and heed what the Spirit says to the churches. To him who [b]overcomes [the world through believing that Jesus is the Son of God], I will grant [the privilege] to eat [the fruit] from the tree of life, which is in the Paradise of God.'*
Message to Smyrna

[8] *"And to the angel (divine messenger) of the church in [c]Smyrna write:*

"These are the words of the First and the Last [absolute Deity, the Son of God] who died and came to life [again]:

Footnotes:

Revelation 2:6 There is scant information about the cult of the Nicolaitans, but it appears they adopted a syncretistic worship, combining Christianity and idolatry. They may have held heretical views similar to those mentioned in vv 14 and 20.

Revelation 2:7 The definition of one who overcomes is recorded in 1 John 5:5.

Revelation 2:8 In ancient times Smyrna (modern Izmir, Turkey) was a beautiful, cosmopolitan city. Located on the Aegean coast, it vied with Ephesus and Pergamum in importance in Asia Minor. It was closely identified with Rome and the cult of emperor worship. Smyrna was later the home of Polycarp, the great Christian church leader who, at the age of eighty-six, was burned at the stake for his refusal to worship the Roman emperor.

REVELATION 20:12-14 KING JAMES VERSION (KJV)

[12] And I saw the dead, small and great, stand before God; and the books were opened: and another book was opened, which is the book of life: and the dead were judged out of those things which were written in the books, according to their works.

[13] And the sea gave up the dead which were in it; and death and hell delivered up the dead which were in them: and they were judged every man according to their works.

[14] And death and hell were cast into the lake of fire. This is the second death.

CHAPTER 7

Eternal Life How do I portray it

L et's consider where we left off in the last chapter. Eternal life is like comparing two different states. One is a condition of living in eternal bliss or one living in eternal pain or unhappiness. The word eternal applies to both. It designates something that continues on forever. It is in this life where we know it will eventually come to an end. We term this as death. The mortal body will die but in eternity the spirit of man lives on forevermore. There will come a time when both body and spirit will be rejoined just as Jesus' body and spirit were rejoined on Easter Sunday. So, we will all have a resurrected body one day.

ECCLESIASTES 3:1-3 KING JAMES VERSION
¹ To every thing there is a season, and a time to every purpose under the heaven:
² A time to be born, and a time to die; a time to plant, and a time to pluck up that which is planted;
³ A time to kill, and a time to heal; a time to break down, and a time to build up;

The medical community defines death (the end of life as we know it) as the cessation of lack of brain activity. So, in our world we see death as a final state. where the body ceases to function. For us this then is the end of everything for when our brain ceases to work for us this is the very end. Nothing can occur because to us the brain is the center of all that we are. It controls all our bodily functions. It is the source of all reasoning and thought and in it resides all our memoires and knowledge. Our senses and all that we value stops. We can no longer have the ability to touch, or smell odors, or taste with our tongue or hear with our eats or see with our eyes. We can no longer have those unidentifiable things like love, hate, anger, joy, happiness, pleasure, sadness, pain, anguish, despair, and hope. These emotions and feelings are all part of us but we are not able to identify how these occur. Yet we have learned that we can physically control some of these. We can perform a lobotomy which is to hack off a section of the brain or use drugs or electrical stimulus to encourage or to discourage these functions and feelings. So, to us in death we cannot any longer experience anything which to us defines existence. To us then, when death occurs or happens everything ceases.

Yet spiritually we have the same senses as those we have experienced in this physical realm. In the spiritual realm we have eternal life and we continue to function. We have spiritual eyes with which we can see the spiritual and physical. We have spiritual touch. We have spiritual thought and knowledge. We have spiritual taste and feel. We have spiritual emotions. We have spiritual ears to hear with. Yes, we even have a spiritual brain which processes and controls the spirit within us. Then there is the immeasurable conscience with we have stored the elements provided from God in which has been stored the essence of what is good and perfect and right and wrong. This exists in each of us in both the physical life and the spiritual life. In it we store all our decisions and actions and all that we do. It provides the compass which can lead us to God or which we can ignore. When we choose to not follow our conscience, we choose to follow our own self will influenced by either the spirit of man or the spirit of the devil or both. Either way we exercise our own self will.

We then come to the point where we need to see what exemplifies eternal life and or eternal death (which is self-condemnation). Eternal life comes about when we repent and believe and accept Jesus as our savior and God as the creator (ruler the source of all creation). Eternal life is the start of our spiritual life with God. It is a beginning of our spiritual birth. It has no end. It is a time of re-learning. When this occurs, we are set on a course where we allow God to bring to pass a combining of the physical and spiritual senses so they agree with those of God. Instead of the flesh being our ruling authority, Jesus by the Holy Spirit brings us to accept God's righteousness as our ruling authority. For some that happens at a much faster pace than it does in others.

ISAIAH 28:9-14 KING JAMES VERSION (KJV)

⁹ Whom shall he teach knowledge? and whom shall he make to understand doctrine? them that are weaned from the milk, and drawn from the breasts.

¹⁰ For precept must be upon precept, precept upon precept; line upon line, line upon line; here a little, and there a little:

¹¹ For with stammering lips and another tongue will he speak to this people.

¹² To whom he said, This is the rest wherewith ye may cause the weary to rest; and this is the refreshing: yet they would not hear.

¹³ But the word of the Lord was unto them precept upon precept, precept upon precept; line upon line, line upon line; here a little, and there a little; that they might go, and fall backward, and be broken, and snared, and taken.

¹⁴ Wherefore hear the word of the Lord, ye scornful men, that rule this people which is in Jerusalem.

1 CHRONICLES 28:8-10 KING JAMES VERSION

⁸ Now therefore in the sight of all Israel the congregation of the Lord, and in the audience of our God, keep and seek for all the commandments of the Lord your God: that ye may possess this good land, and leave it for an inheritance for your children after you for ever.

⁹ And thou, Solomon my son, know thou the God of thy father, and serve him with a perfect heart and with a willing mind: for the Lord searcheth all hearts, and understandeth all the imaginations of the thoughts: if thou seek him, he will be found of thee; but if thou forsake him, he will cast thee off for ever.

¹⁰ Take heed now; for the Lord hath chosen thee to build an house for the sanctuary: be strong, and do it.

PSALM 10:3-5 KING JAMES VERSION

³ For the wicked boasteth of his heart's desire, and blesseth the covetous, whom the Lord abhorreth.

⁴ The wicked, through the pride of his countenance, will not seek after God: God is not in all his thoughts.

⁵ His ways are always grievous; thy judgments are far above out of his sight: as for all his enemies, he puffeth at them.

The first step in this process has and always will be God's will to bring all human kind into His fold to dwell with Him. He continues to try to encourage us to see that His ways are best. When we choose to accept this then He can go about the task of first transforming our spiritual senses to work in the same way His does.

ISAIAH 55:8-13 KING JAMES VERSION

8 For my thoughts are not your thoughts, neither are your ways my ways, saith the Lord.

9 For as the heavens are higher than the earth, so are my ways higher than your ways, and my thoughts than your thoughts.

10 For as the rain cometh down, and the snow from heaven, and returneth not thither, but watereth the earth, and maketh it bring forth and bud, that it may give seed to the sower, and bread to the eater:

11 So shall my word be that goeth forth out of my mouth: it shall not return unto me void, but it shall accomplish that which I please, and it shall prosper in the thing whereto I sent it.

12 For ye shall go out with joy, and be led forth with peace: the mountains and the hills shall break forth before you into singing, and all the trees of the field shall clap their hands.

13 Instead of the thorn shall come up the fir tree, and instead of the brier shall come up the myrtle tree: and it shall be to the Lord for a name, for an everlasting sign that shall not be cut off.

So, to put it into plain English, He works with us pointing out where we have allowed the wrong things to control us and teaching us how to reverse these into the right things. Sinful things limit our potential. They prevent us from being all we were created to be. They limit the potential to truly know what everlasting joy peace and happiness are and what is truly of value and worth experiencing for eternity.

Eternal life is experiencing the benefit of following God and His ways and having them as part of our makeup. We now can experience all things in the way they were created to be experienced. It is a relearning of what the creation is and how we fit into it and it is a relearning of why and who we were created to be. We were raised by our earthly parents on earth from our beginning. In eternity we are adopted by our heavenly parents and we are taught by them.

JUDGES 13:7-25 KING JAMES VERSION (KJV)

7 But he said unto me, Behold, thou shalt conceive, and bear a son; and now drink no wine nor strong drink, neither eat any unclean thing: for the child shall be a Nazarite to God from the womb to the day of his death.

[8] Then Manoah intreated the Lord, and said, O my Lord, let the man of God which thou didst send come again unto us, and teach us what we shall do unto the child that shall be born.

[9] And God hearkened to the voice of Manoah; and the angel of God came again unto the woman as she sat in the field: but Manoah her husband was not with her.

[10] And the woman made haste, and ran, and shewed her husband, and said unto him, Behold, the man hath appeared unto me, that came unto me the other day.

[11] And Manoah arose, and went after his wife, and came to the man, and said unto him, Art thou the man that spakest unto the woman? And he said, I am.

[12] And Manoah said, Now let thy words come to pass. How shall we order the child, and how shall we do unto him?

[13] And the angel of the Lord said unto Manoah, Of all that I said unto the woman let her beware.

[14] She may not eat of any thing that cometh of the vine, neither let her drink wine or strong drink, nor eat any unclean thing: all that I commanded her let her observe.

[15] And Manoah said unto the angel of the Lord, I pray thee, let us detain thee, until we shall have made ready a kid for thee.

[16] And the angel of the Lord said unto Manoah, Though thou detain me, I will not eat of thy bread: and if thou wilt offer a burnt offering, thou must offer it unto the Lord. For Manoah knew not that he was an angel of the Lord.

[17] And Manoah said unto the angel of the Lord, What is thy name, that when thy sayings come to pass we may do thee honour?

[18] And the angel of the Lord said unto him, Why askest thou thus after my name, seeing it is secret?

[19] So Manoah took a kid with a meat offering, and offered it upon a rock unto the Lord: and the angel did wonderously; and Manoah and his wife looked on.

[20] For it came to pass, when the flame went up toward heaven from off the altar, that the angel of the Lord ascended in the flame of the altar. And Manoah and his wife looked on it, and fell on their faces to the ground.

[21] But the angel of the Lord did no more appear to Manoah and to his wife. Then Manoah knew that he was an angel of the Lord.

[22] And Manoah said unto his wife, We shall surely die, because we have seen God.

[23] But his wife said unto him, If the Lord were pleased to kill us, he would not have received a burnt offering and a meat offering at

our hands, neither would he have shewed us all these things, nor would as at this time have told us such things as these.

²⁴ And the woman bare a son, and called his name Samson: and the child grew, and the Lord blessed him.

JOHN 3:2-15 AMPLIFIED BIBLE (AMP)

² who came to Jesus at night and said to Him, "Rabbi (Teacher), we know [without any doubt] that You have come from God as a teacher; for no one can do these signs [these wonders, these attesting miracles] that You do unless God is with him."

³ Jesus answered him, "I assure you and most solemnly say to you, unless a person is born again [reborn from above—spiritually transformed, renewed, sanctified], he cannot [ever] see and experience the kingdom of God."

⁴ Nicodemus said to Him, "How can a man be born when he is old? He cannot enter his mother's womb a second time and be born, can he?"

⁵ Jesus answered, "I assure you and most solemnly say to you, unless one is born of water and the Spirit he cannot [ever] enter the kingdom of God.

⁶ That which is born of the flesh is flesh [the physical is merely physical], and that which is born of the Spirit is spirit.

⁷ Do not be surprised that I have told you, 'You must be born again [reborn from above—spiritually transformed, renewed, sanctified].'

⁸ The wind blows where it wishes and you hear its sound, but you do not know where it is coming from and where it is going; so it is with everyone who is born of the Spirit."

⁹ Nicodemus said to Him, "How can these things be possible?"

¹⁰ Jesus replied, "You are the [great and well-known] teacher of Israel, and yet you do not know nor understand these things [from Scripture]?

¹¹ I assure you and most solemnly say to you, we speak only of what we [absolutely] know and testify about what we have [actually] seen [as eyewitnesses]; and [still] you [reject our evidence and] do not accept our testimony.

¹² If I told you earthly things [that is, things that happen right here on earth] and you do not believe, how will you believe and trust Me if I tell you heavenly things?

¹³ No one has gone up into heaven, but there is One who came down from heaven, the Son of Man [Himself—whose home is in heaven].

14 Just as Moses lifted up the [bronze] serpent in the desert [on a pole], so must the Son of Man be lifted up [on the cross],
15 so that whoever believes will in Him have eternal life [after physical death, and will actually live forever].

Our earthly parents do not have a clue as to how to raise us spiritually and even when following scripture or an angel we make mistakes which we pass on. The scripture above shows that although Samson and Nicodemus were born many years apart each had many of the same limitations.

Summary

In eternity we become as a baby who has to learn to use the body and senses he has been provided to perceive and use the creation around him for the good for which it was originally intended.

GALATIANS 3:25-27 AMPLIFIED BIBLE (AMP)
25 But now that faith has come, we are no longer under [the control and authority of] a tutor and disciplinarian.
26 For you [who are born-again have been reborn from above— spiritually transformed, renewed, sanctified and] are all children of God [set apart for His purpose with full rights and privileges] through faith in Christ Jesus.
27 For all of you who were baptized into Christ [into a spiritual union with the Christ, the Anointed] have clothed yourselves with Christ [that is, you have taken on His characteristics and values].

We hear many Christians use this phrase but do they really understand what is meant by it? I am led to use a baby and its discovery of life to demonstrate being born again. To be born again is like becoming a baby again in that we must start learning anew the elements of our world. Have you ever seen how a baby discovers how to control its body we must learn how to control and use the attributes of our spirit under the tutelage of the one true Father? Just as a baby discovers he/she has hands which he can control or feet with which when used with his legs, arms and the rest of his body to walk. Just as a baby learns to talk and comprehend speech. We too who walk in eternity start over with the basics at baptism or we when we first believed (repented and accepted God and Jesus) and move on to each progressive point in the life to live with God. Instead of being taught how to live by a set of earthly parents we are taught under the guidance of the Father and Son by the Holy Spirit to live just as God wants us to.

ISAIAH 28:9-14 KING JAMES VERSION (KJV)

9 Whom shall he teach knowledge? and whom shall he make to understand doctrine? them that are weaned from the milk, and drawn from the breasts.

10 For precept must be upon precept, precept upon precept; line upon line, line upon line; here a little, and there a little:

11 For with stammering lips and another tongue will he speak to this people.

12 To whom he said, This is the rest wherewith ye may cause the weary to rest; and this is the refreshing: yet they would not hear.

13 But the word of the Lord was unto them precept upon precept, precept upon precept; line upon line, line upon line; here a little, and there a little; that they might go, and fall backward, and be broken, and snared, and taken.

14 Wherefore hear the word of the Lord, ye scornful men, that rule this people which is in Jerusalem.

We start at a point of rebirth where all things become new and we are transformed from a state of being controlled by our sinful nature to a new nature controlled by God's righteousness and His divine design. New in that we haven't been using the right methods to think and use our being in the way it was originally oriented to be. Think how a baby comes into this world dependent on his parents to care for him and protect him. We in eternity learn this same way. We look to our parents to protect us and teach all the elemental things. Then it is up to us to choose how learn to use the value of the experiences of life are showing us with a mind controlled by a new outlook on the value of the conscience God has provided.

1 JOHN 3:8-10 AMPLIFIED BIBLE (AMP)

8 The one who practices sin [separating himself from God, and offending Him by acts of disobedience, indifference, or rebellion] is of the devil [and takes his inner character and moral values from him, not God]; for the devil has sinned and violated God's law from the beginning. The Son of God appeared for this purpose, to destroy the works of the devil.

9 No one who is born of God [deliberately, knowingly, and habitually] practices sin, because [a]God's seed [His principle of life, the essence of His righteous character] remains [permanently] in him [who is born again—who is reborn from above—spiritually transformed, renewed, and set apart for His purpose]; and he [who is born again] cannot habitually [live a life characterized by] sin, because he is born of God and longs to please Him.

10 By this the children of God and the children of the devil are clearly identified: anyone who does not practice righteousness [who does not seek God's will in thought, action, and purpose] is not of God, nor is the one who does not [unselfishly] [b]love his [believing] brother.

Footnotes:

1 John 3:9 I.e. in human terms, God's seed is like a divine "genetic code" which is passed on to His children and produces in them the desire to live in a way which pleases Him.

1 John 3:10 See note 2:10.

1 John 2:10 The key to understanding this and other statements about love is to know that this love (the Greek word agape) is not so much a matter of emotion as it is of doing things for the benefit of another person, that is, having an unselfish concern for another and a willingness to seek the best for another.

We learn to see that those things in our conscience were placed there for our good. We learn that we can trust those things He has placed there. So, we relearn to use them to make good choices and we become the embodiment of God here on earth and in the heaven which lies ahead. That is why in scripture we are told we must be born again and to move from acting like a new baby and eventual move into the mature state of being with Christ as our head walking in the Spirit. Jesus along with the Holy Spirit starts this process and continues with it until we come to be the way were originally created to be. We learn how to walk in true love and make choices based on Godly love and not just human emotion. The final result is that we will become perfect, in the similitude of Christ Jesus.

1 CORINTHIANS 13:1-10 KING JAMES VERSION

1 Though I speak with the tongues of men and of angels, and have not charity, I am become as sounding brass, or a tinkling cymbal.

2 And though I have the gift of prophecy, and understand all mysteries, and all knowledge; and though I have all faith, so that I could remove mountains, and have not charity, I am nothing.

3 And though I bestow all my goods to feed the poor, and though I give my body to be burned, and have not charity, it profiteth me nothing.

4 Charity suffereth long, and is kind; charity envieth not; charity vaunteth not itself, is not puffed up,

5 Doth not behave itself unseemly, seeketh not her own, is not easily provoked, thinketh no evil;

6 Rejoiceth not in iniquity, but rejoiceth in the truth;

7 Beareth all things, believeth all things, hopeth all things, endureth all things.

8 Charity never faileth: but whether there be prophecies, they shall fail; whether there be tongues, they shall cease; whether there be knowledge, it shall vanish away.

9 For we know in part, and we prophesy in part.

10 But when that which is perfect is come, then that which is in part shall be done away. Though I speak with the tongues of men and of angels, and have not charity, I am become as sounding brass, or a tinkling cymbal.

JAMES 1:1-27 AMPLIFIED BIBLE (AMP)

Testing Your Faith

1 [a]James, a bond-servant of God and of the Lord Jesus Christ,

To the twelve [Hebrew] tribes [scattered abroad among the Gentiles] in the dispersion: Greetings (rejoice)!

2 Consider it nothing but joy, my [b]brothers and sisters, whenever you fall into various trials.

3 Be assured that the testing of your faith [through experience] produces endurance [leading to spiritual maturity, and inner peace].

4 And let endurance have its perfect result and do a thorough work, so that you may be perfect and completely developed [in your faith], lacking in nothing.

5 If any of you lacks wisdom [to guide him through a decision or circumstance], he is to ask of [our benevolent] God, who gives to everyone generously and without rebuke or blame, and it will be given to him.

6 But he must ask [for wisdom] in faith, without doubting [God's willingness to help], for the one who doubts is like a billowing surge of the sea that is blown about and tossed by the wind.

7 For such a person ought not to think or expect that he will receive anything [at all] from the Lord,

8 being a double-minded man, unstable and restless in all his ways [in everything he thinks, feels, or decides].

9 Let the brother in humble circumstances glory in his high position [as a born-again believer, called to the true riches and to be an heir of God];

¹⁰ and the rich man is to glory in being humbled [by trials revealing human frailty, knowing true riches are found in the grace of God], for like the flower of the grass he will pass away.

¹¹ For the sun rises with a scorching wind and withers the grass; its flower falls off and [c]its beauty fades away; so too will the rich man, in the midst of his pursuits, fade away.

¹² Blessed [happy, spiritually prosperous, favored by God] is the man who is steadfast under trial and perseveres when tempted; for when he has passed the test and been approved, he will receive the [victor's] crown of life which the Lord has promised to those who love Him.

¹³ Let no one say when he is tempted, "I am being tempted by God" [for temptation does not originate from God, but from our own flaws]; for God cannot be tempted by [what is] evil, and He Himself tempts no one.

¹⁴ But each one is tempted when he is dragged away, enticed and baited [to commit sin] by his own [worldly] desire (lust, passion). ¹⁵ Then when the illicit desire has conceived, it gives birth to sin; and when sin has run its course, it gives birth to death.

¹⁶ Do not be misled, my beloved brothers and sisters.

¹⁷ Every good thing given and every perfect gift is from above; it comes down from the Father of lights [the Creator and Sustainer of the heavens], in whom there is no variation [no rising or setting] or shadow [d]cast by His turning [for He is perfect and never changes].

¹⁸ It was of His own will that He gave us birth [as His children] by the word of truth, so that we would be a kind of first fruits of His creatures [a prime example of what He created to be set apart to Himself—sanctified, made holy for His divine purposes].

¹⁹ Understand this, my beloved brothers and sisters. Let everyone be quick to hear [be a careful, thoughtful listener], slow to speak [a speaker of carefully chosen words and], slow to anger [patient, reflective, forgiving];

²⁰ for the [resentful, deep-seated] anger of man does not produce the righteousness of God [that standard of behavior which He requires from us].

²¹ So get rid of all uncleanness and [e]all that remains of wickedness, and with a humble spirit receive the word [of God] which is implanted [actually rooted in your heart], which is able to save your souls.

²² But prove yourselves doers of the word [actively and continually obeying God's precepts], and not merely listeners [who hear the

word but fail to internalize its meaning], deluding yourselves [by unsound reasoning contrary to the truth].

23 For if anyone only listens to the word [f]without obeying it, he is like a man who looks very carefully at his natural face in a mirror; 24 for once he has looked at himself and gone away, he immediately forgets [g]what he looked like.

25 But he who looks carefully into the perfect law, the law of liberty, and faithfully abides by it, not having become a [careless] listener who forgets but [h]an active doer [who obeys], he will be blessed and favored by God in what he does [in his life of obedience].

26 If anyone thinks himself to be religious [scrupulously observant of the rituals of his faith], and does not control his tongue but deludes his own heart, this person's religion is worthless (futile, barren).

27 Pure and unblemished religion [as it is expressed in outward acts] in the sight of our God and Father is this: to visit and look after the fatherless and the widows in their distress, and to keep oneself uncontaminated by the [secular] world.

The state of Eternal life is one of learning and rejuvenation. Where all things become new and old things are cast away. Cast away in the sense of being replaced with things of eternal value. This is when those things which are worthless or of no redeeming consequence are no longer part of our nature. They are then replaced with those things which exemplify God become part of us. Yes, for some we start over completely learning and reorienting the direction of our lives. This allows the restructured choices in our lives to be in line with those of God for the good of all. We then will be in line with God's laws and principles that He made part of His creation. The statement of Jesus in which He said we must be born again becomes a reality. We then mature into being like Jesus: thinking, doing, seeing, saying, choosing, and wanting only those things we see the Father do. You see we have always had the free will to choose between the good and the bad. Man's dilemma and hope all are expressed in the following passage. It describes, if you prayerfully read it, how we reason and why we need God's help. I choose to use the Amplified Bible translation as it translates from the original manuscript sources using a more modern usage of the word "eternal" in verse 3:11, instead of the word "world" as in the King James version. This is the same as most modern translations use.

ECCLESIASTES 3:1-22 AMPLIFIED BIBLE

A Time for Everything

¹ *There is a season (a time appointed) for everything and a time for every delight and event or purpose under heaven—*
² *A time to be born and a time to die;*
A time to plant and a time to uproot what is planted.
³ *A time to kill and a time to heal;*
A time to tear down and a time to build up.
⁴ *A time to weep and a time to laugh;*
A time to mourn and a time to dance.
⁵ *A time to throw away stones and a time to gather stones;*
A time to embrace and a time to refrain from embracing.
⁶ *A time to search and a time to give up as lost;*
A time to keep and a time to throw away.
⁷ *A time to [a]tear apart and a time to sew together;*
A time to keep silent and a time to speak.
⁸ *A time to love and a time to hate;*
A time for war and a time for peace.
⁹ *What profit is there for the worker from that in which he labors?*
¹⁰ *I have seen the task which God has given to the sons of men with which to occupy themselves.*

God Set Eternity in the Heart of Man

¹¹ *He has made everything beautiful and appropriate in its time. He has also planted eternity [a sense of divine purpose] in the human heart [a mysterious longing which nothing under the sun can satisfy, except God]—yet man cannot find out (comprehend, grasp) what God has done (His overall plan) from the beginning to the end.*
¹² *I know that there is nothing better for them than to rejoice and to do good as long as they live;*
¹³ *and also that every man should eat and drink and see and enjoy the good of all his labor—it is the gift of God.*
¹⁴ *I know that whatever God does, it endures forever; nothing can be added to it nor can anything be taken from it, for God does it so that men will fear and worship Him [with awe-filled reverence, knowing that He is God].*
¹⁵ *That which is has already been, and that which will be has already been, for God seeks what has passed by [so that history repeats itself].*
¹⁶ *Moreover, I have seen under the sun that in the place of justice there is wickedness, and in the place of righteousness there is wickedness.*

[17] I said to myself, "God will judge both the righteous and the wicked," for there is a time [appointed] for every matter and for every deed.

[18] I said to myself regarding the sons of men, "God is surely testing them in order for them to see that [by themselves, without God] they are [only] animals."

[19] For the [earthly] fate of the sons of men and the fate of animals is the same. As one dies, so dies the other; indeed, they all have the same breath and there is no preeminence or advantage for man [in and of himself] over an animal, for all is vanity.

[20] All go to the same place. All came from the dust and all return to the dust.

[21] Who knows if the spirit of man ascends upward and the spirit of the animal descends downward to the earth?

[22] So I have seen that there is nothing better than that a man should be happy in his own works and activities, for that is his portion (share). For who will bring him [back] to see what will happen after he is gone?

Footnotes

Ecclesiastes 3:7 This may be a reference to the practice of tearing one's clothes as a sign of mourning which began early among the Hebrews. Cf Gen 37:29. There are many references to this in the Old Testament. Solomon was no doubt familiar with this practice as his own father engaged in it with his contemporaries. Cf 2 Sam 3:31.

CHAPTER 8

Eternal Life Vs This Life

Scripture introduces us to life as God created. Man, in his viewpoint only has a limited sense of life, which to him ends in death. This is because if you only go by reason and our knowledge based on our senses that is all you can grasp even though the world around us leads us to understand there is more than a few years to existence of all things. You see we limit ourselves or we allow our self-image to be expanded through the observation of God's creation or to be blinded by our refusal to accept God and a creation which extends far beyond our understanding.

ROMANS 1:15-21 KING JAMES VERSION

¹⁵ So, as much as in me is, I am ready to preach the gospel to you that are at Rome also.

¹⁶ For I am not ashamed of the gospel of Christ: for it is the power of God unto salvation to every one that believeth; to the Jew first, and also to the Greek.

¹⁷ For therein is the righteousness of God revealed from faith to faith: as it is written, The just shall live by faith.

¹⁸ For the wrath of God is revealed from heaven against all ungodliness and unrighteousness of men, who hold the truth in unrighteousness;

¹⁹ Because that which may be known of God is manifest in them; for God hath shewed it unto them.

²⁰ For the invisible things of him from the creation of the world are clearly seen, being understood by the things that are made, even his eternal power and Godhead; so that they are without excuse:

²¹ Because that, when they knew God, they glorified him not as God, neither were thankful; but became vain in their imaginations, and their foolish heart was darkened.

We use all the principles on which the creation is based to guide our science or our identity. You see we base everything on time. We are guided by clocks, seasons and the day to day existence which we have been taught from generation to generation. Daily we see men and women die and placed in graves. We have come to a point just as stated in the understanding presented in the book of Ecclesiastes. That is, there is no true understanding of what this life is about other than self-indulgence. In the book of Ecclesiastes, it is stated that life is something difficult to understand. We cannot seem to grasp its meaning other than the fact we live from minute to minute until the end comes. For the most part we try to ignore or not keep in mind that the universe around us has intelligent origin. In our human thought patterns, we are bombarded with theories of how we came into being. We have many who are acclaimed for their knowledge and promote all these theories in a manner that we can accept. We are then inclined to put our trust in them rather than the scriptural and natural evidence which abounds all around us that provide proof of the existence of God. We have so many theories from Darwinism to modern day science's big bang to theories of aliens from outer space which was the start of our existence. Each of these tries to explain away the intelligence behind how and why this creation came about. We don't want to accept anything that we can't experience with our senses or we can't explain other than by our intellect, labeled as science. Yet, none of these touches on the reason for our existence and how we are to live other than survival of the fittest. Some animals around like the lion or tiger do this but we are not animals. We have choice. We have the choice to live like some of them who live for the good of the whole, just as the bees and ants do. Some even try to come up with an explanation of life but we seem to try to be either drawn to create our own gods trying to fulfill an inner need to grasp on to why. Why are we here? Why do things happen the way that they do? Why can't we control everything? Why do I exist and what should my goals be or the who or what? Who are we and what is to become of us? What defines our goals should be or where are we headed? So, we are drawn in many different directions by philosophy or by just self-preservation or by just live and let live or to create our own religion to compensate for all the things we cannot explain. We then choose to live by our wits or to live by the divine. Living by our wits leads to the only reason for existence is us and our own self pleasure and to ignore those things which are beyond our physical senses or which we cannot explain. So, this life leaves us with a choice. To follow only that which we can handle or understand or to fulfill that unexplainable thing within which draws us to choose the true God or the devil or to follow our selfish nature. Let's survey the following scriptures.

PROVERBS 21:2 KING JAMES VERSION
2 Every way of a man is right in his own eyes: but the Lord pondereth the hearts.

LUKE 6:43-45 AMPLIFIED BIBLE
43 For there is no good tree which produces bad fruit, nor, on the other hand, a bad tree which produces good fruit.
44 For each tree is known and identified by its own fruit. For figs are not picked from thorn bushes, nor is a cluster of grapes picked from a briar bush.
45 The [intrinsically] good man produces what is good and honorable and moral out of the good treasure [stored] in his heart; and the [intrinsically] evil man produces what is wicked and depraved out of the evil [in his heart]; for his mouth speaks from the overflow of his heart.

JEREMIAH 9:13-15 KING JAMES VERSION (KJV)
13 And the Lord saith, Because they have forsaken my law which I set before them, and have not obeyed my voice, neither walked therein;
14 But have walked after the imagination of their own heart, and after Baalim, which their fathers taught them:
15 Therefore thus saith the Lord of hosts, the God of Israel; Behold, I will feed them, even this people, with wormwood, and give them water of gall to drink

Our humanism is exemplified in scripture by the thoughts of Eve in the garden as she is approached by the devil. She was led to use her reasoning skills to make a choice based on her physical sense of sight, taste, self-glorification (inner desires) and her ability to reject the knowledge of what she thought she had been taught and that inner voice within (her conscience). The devil was able to convince her it was for her best good to do what she deemed as acceptable for her rather than accept what God had said. She was being encouraged to ignore that inner sense of right and wrong and to just follow her own instincts. She was led to consider that if it looks good or sounds good or seems to be more for my own benefit and I am incomplete without it, then why not do it? She was led to reason that just because God said it that it was not necessarily true. She was led to use her own will to override the will of God. She was led to place her reasoning above the council of God and to accept she was incomplete without the forbidden fruit. This is the same approach used by modern day advertisement philosophy. Let's look at this in scripture.

GENESIS 3:1-14 KING JAMES VERSION

¹ Now the serpent was more subtil than any beast of the field which the Lord God had made. And he said unto the woman, Yea, hath ᴳᵒᵈ said, Ye shall not eat of every tree of the garden?

² And the woman said unto the serpent, We may eat of the fruit of the trees of the garden:

³ But of the fruit of the tree which is in the midst of the garden, God hath said, Ye shall not eat of it, neither shall ye touch it, lest ye die.

⁴ And the serpent said unto the woman, Ye shall not surely die:

⁵ For God doth know that in the day ye eat thereof, then your eyes shall be opened, and ye shall be as gods, knowing good and evil.

⁶ And when the woman saw that the tree was good for food, and that it was pleasant to the eyes, and a tree to be desired to make one wise, she took of the fruit thereof, and did eat, and gave also unto her husband with her; and he did eat.

⁷ And the eyes of them both were opened, and they knew that they were naked; and they sewed fig leaves together, and made themselves aprons.

⁸ And they heard the voice of the Lord God walking in the garden in the cool of the day: and Adam and his wife hid themselves from the presence of the Lord God amongst the trees of the garden.

⁹ And the Lord God called unto Adam, and said unto him, Where art thou?

¹⁰ And he said, I heard thy voice in the garden, and I was afraid, because I was naked; and I hid myself.

¹¹ And he said, Who told thee that thou wast naked? Hast thou eaten of the tree, whereof I commanded thee that thou shouldest not eat?

¹² And the man said, The woman whom thou gavest to be with me, she gave me of the tree, and I did eat.

¹³ And the Lord God said unto the woman, What is this that thou hast done? And the woman said, The serpent beguiled me, and I did eat.

¹⁴ And the Lord God said unto the serpent, Because thou hast done this, thou art cursed above all cattle, and above every beast of the field; upon thy belly shalt thou go, and dust shalt thou eat all the days of thy life:

2 CORINTHIANS 11:3 AMPLIFIED BIBLE (AMP)

[3] *But I am afraid that, even as the serpent beguiled Eve by his cunning, your minds may be corrupted and led away from the simplicity of [your sincere and] pure devotion to Christ.*

Summary

Our inclination is to put this life, which is limited, first in our choices. We follow our selfish nature which only leads to death. Our vision is limited and we are blind to those things eternal. It's just like the fact that the water which falls from the sky has existed since the beginning of this creation yet we see it as a passing thing and don't consider that it will be here as long as this world exists. It is the same water which Adam and Eve had to drink and bathe in. It is the same water which our great, great, great grandkids will have to drink. We take it for granted and don't consider that we need to use it with care and be mindful of polluting it. The air we breathe is the same way. As long as it serves our immediate purposes, we don't consider the long-term impact of our choices. In my training as an engineer I was not taught the need to consider the environmental impact of the chemical processes or the natural laws which we had been taught. We were led to believe that the solution to pollution was dilution. In other words, it will care for itself. This is the approach used until just recent days we figured out that we needed to remove pollutants from our wastes. We were taught that we were to create things which benefit man using the laws and principle of science and math. Yes, we were taught to consider the benefit of man not God's creation.

The Lord has provided that the oxygen in the air to be replenished by trees and plants yet we have taken this for granted and use both trees and the air without recognizing how we impact them in the long term or how it will impact them and mankind over the long term. Yes, we ignore the fact that there is something to be considered beyond our immediate pleasure or selfishness goals.

Our existence has meaning yet we do seem to recognize it. We don't seem to understand that we exist here for a reason. We reason that we are the only part of creation which matters. We see all things as temporary even our existence. Thank God for those who are wakening to the truth.

Our lives continue on without end and will not perish as those things which man has made. You see civilizations come and go but life was established from the beginning and will have no end. Therefore, we either end up in eternal life (living forever with God under His authority) or we will live in eternal punishment (which is death). God has appointed unto man to die once and then to be resurrected again at some future date. We can't measure this so we really don't accept this. Even many of those who have accepted Jesus as their savoir struggle with death and morn at its approach.

ECCLESIASTES 7:1 KING JAMES VERSION

7 A good name is better than precious ointment; and the day of death than the day of one's birth

JOHN 11:30-44 KING JAMES VERSION

30 Now Jesus was not yet come into the town, but was in that place where Martha met him.

31 The Jews then which were with her in the house, and comforted her, when they saw Mary, that she rose up hastily and went out, followed her, saying, She goeth unto the grave to weep there.

32 Then when Mary was come where Jesus was, and saw him, she fell down at his feet, saying unto him, Lord, if thou hadst been here, my brother had not died.

33 When Jesus therefore saw her weeping, and the Jews also weeping which came with her, he groaned in the spirit, and was troubled.

34 And said, Where have ye laid him? They said unto him, Lord, come and see.

35 Jesus wept.

36 Then said the Jews, Behold how he loved him!

37 And some of them said, Could not this man, which opened the eyes of the blind, have caused that even this man should not have died?

38 Jesus therefore again groaning in himself cometh to the grave. It was a cave, and a stone lay upon it.

39 Jesus said, Take ye away the stone. Martha, the sister of him that was dead, saith unto him, Lord, by this time he stinketh: for he hath been dead four days.

40 Jesus saith unto her, Said I not unto thee, that, if thou wouldest believe, thou shouldest see the glory of God?

41 Then they took away the stone from the place where the dead was laid. And Jesus lifted up his eyes, and said, Father, I thank thee that thou hast heard me.
42 And I knew that thou hearest me always: but because of the people which stand by I said it, that they may believe that thou hast sent me.
43 And when he thus had spoken, he cried with a loud voice, Lazarus, come forth.
44 And he that was dead came forth, bound hand and foot with graveclothes: and his face was bound about with a napkin. Jesus saith unto them, Loose him, and let him go.

We have to come to understand that a reorientation of our thinking is needed to grasp eternal life and its implications. Thanks be to God who in His wisdom has a plan for this which will never change and is perfect in every respect. We were created as eternal beings. Yet we don't relate this to ourselves. Temporal death has caused us to lose site of this. We see death as an end of all things. Which is not so. God has instituted temporal death to keep us from feeling we are forced into accepting Him. We were formed to be in the image of God who is eternal. Our eternal existence is based on our God given choice. We have the choice of Eternal Life or eternal punishment. Eternal life is a choice to live forever in the image of God. When we choose life without God, it is a choice to end in eternal punishment which is the second death.

Stopped here

JOSHUA 7:18-20 KING JAMES VERSION (KJV)
18 And he brought his household man by man; and Achan, the son of Carmi, the son of Zabdi, the son of Zerah, of the tribe of Judah, was taken.
19 And Joshua said unto Achan, My son, give, I pray thee, glory to the Lord God of Israel, and make confession unto him; and tell me now what thou hast done; hide it not from me.
20 And Achan answered Joshua, and said, Indeed I have sinned against the Lord God of Israel, and thus and thus have I done:

2 CORINTHIANS 11:1-10 AMPLIFIED BIBLE
Paul Defends His Apostleship
1 I wish you would bear with me [while I indulge] in a little foolishness; but indeed you are bearing with me [as you read this].
2 I am jealous for you with a godly jealousy because I have promised you to one husband, to present you as a pure virgin to Christ.

3 But I am afraid that, even as the serpent beguiled Eve by his cunning, your minds may be corrupted and led away from the simplicity of [your sincere and] pure devotion to Christ.

4 For [you seem willing to allow it] if one comes and preaches another Jesus whom we have not preached, or if you receive a different spirit from the one you received, or a different gospel from the one you accepted. You tolerate all this beautifully [welcoming the deception].

5 Yet I consider myself in no way inferior to the [so-called] [a]super-apostles.

6 But even if I am unskilled in speaking, yet I am not [untrained] in [b]knowledge [I know what I am talking about]; but we have made this evident to you in every way, in all things.

7 Or did I [perhaps] sin by humbling myself so that you might be exalted and honored, because I preached God's gospel to you [c]free of charge?

8 I robbed other churches by accepting [more than their share of] financial support for my ministry to you.

9 And when I was with you and ran short [financially], I did not burden any of you; for what I needed was fully supplied by the brothers (Silas and Timothy) who came from Macedonia (the church at Philippi). So I kept myself from being a burden to you in any way, and will continue to do so.

10 As the truth of Christ is in me, my boast [of independence] will not be silenced in the regions of Achaia (southern Greece).

Footnotes

2 Corinthians 11:5 This may be a sarcastic reference to the teachers of false doctrine (pseudo-apostles) who opposed Paul and tried to claim they had an association with the original twelve disciples.

2 Corinthians 11:6 Like the original Twelve, Paul received his knowledge of the gospel from the Lord.

2 Corinthians 11:7 Traveling philosophers and religious teachers (including the false apostles) customarily charged for their lectures. Paul's reason for refusing support from this church is unclear.

Just as the devil told Eve to question God, we do the same. We don't walk around thinking well I am going to die someday so I need to prepare for this. Or should I believe that death will come. Most of us approach life on the premise that tomorrow will come and to ignore the fact that this body will someday cease to function. We know we can choose to live a mundane existence or just call it to an end and commit suicide. Either way we are lying to ourselves and we are dead to God in spirit and in truth. So, in this life, which is a learning experience, we learn to follow God and His original plan or we learn to ignore the existence of God and choose to live a life apart from Him.

PROVERBS 9:8-10 KING JAMES VERSION (KJV)

8 Reprove not a scorner, lest he hate thee: rebuke a wise man, and he will love thee.

9 Give instruction to a wise man, and he will be yet wiser: teach a just man, and he will increase in learning.

10 The fear of the Lord is the beginning of wisdom: and the knowledge of the holy is understanding.

DANIEL 1:16-17 KING JAMES VERSION (KJV)

16 Thus Melzar took away the portion of their meat, and the wine that they should drink; and gave them pulse.

17 As for these four children, God gave them knowledge and skill in all learning and wisdom: and Daniel had understanding in all visions and dreams.

ROMANS 15:3-5 KING JAMES VERSION (KJV)

3 For even Christ pleased not himself; but, as it is written, The reproaches of them that reproached thee fell on me.

4 For whatsoever things were written aforetime were written for our learning, that we through patience and comfort of the scriptures might have hope.

5 Now the God of patience and consolation grant you to be likeminded one toward another according to Christ Jesus:

2 TIMOTHY 3:8-10 KING JAMES VERSION (KJV)

8 Now as Jannes and Jambres withstood Moses, so do these also resist the truth: men of corrupt minds, reprobate concerning the faith.

9 But they shall proceed no further: for their folly shall be manifest unto all men, as their's also was.

10 But thou hast fully known my doctrine, manner of life, purpose, faith, longsuffering, charity, patience,

2 TIMOTHY 3:8-10 AMPLIFIED BIBLE (AMP)

8 Just as Jannes and Jambres [the court magicians of Egypt] opposed Moses, so these men also oppose the truth, men of depraved mind, unqualified and worthless [as teachers] in regard to the faith.

9 But they will not get very far, for their meaningless nonsense and ignorance will become obvious to everyone, as was that of Jannes and Jambres.

¹⁰ Now you have diligently followed [my example, that is] my teaching, conduct, purpose, faith, patience, love, steadfastness,

As a born-again believer we start learning all over. We learn to cast away the chains of sinful ways and learn to choose the righteousness of God. We start with line upon line and precept upon precept until we reach the fullness of understanding of Christ Jesus and God the Father or until we are satisfied with the way we are and are unwilling to move any further. This is the work of the Holy Spirit in us, teaching as we allow or accept it, to release us from the old self and transform us into the image of Christ Jesus.

ISAIAH 28:9-11 KING JAMES VERSION (KJV)

⁹ Whom shall he teach knowledge? and whom shall he make to understand doctrine? them that are weaned from the milk, and drawn from the breasts.

¹⁰ For precept must be upon precept, precept upon precept; line upon line, line upon line; here a little, and there a little:

¹¹ For with stammering lips and another tongue will he speak to this people.

ROMANS 2:6-12 KING JAMES VERSION (KJV)

⁶ Who will render to every man according to his deeds:

⁷ To them who by patient continuance in well doing seek for glory and honour and immortality, eternal life:

⁸ But unto them that are contentious, and do not obey the truth, but obey unrighteousness, indignation and wrath,

⁹ Tribulation and anguish, upon every soul of man that doeth evil, of the Jew first, and also of the Gentile;

¹⁰ But glory, honour, and peace, to every man that worketh good, to the Jew first, and also to the Gentile:

¹¹ For there is no respect of persons with God.

¹² For as many as have sinned without law shall also perish without law: and as many as have sinned in the law shall be judged by the law;

2 CORINTHIANS 3:17-18 KING JAMES VERSION (KJV)

¹⁷ Now the Lord is that Spirit: and where the Spirit of the Lord is, there is liberty.

¹⁸ But we all, with open face beholding as in a glass the glory of the Lord, are changed into the same image from glory to glory, even as by the Spirit of the Lord.

2 CORINTHIANS 3:17-18 AMPLIFIED BIBLE (AMP)

¹⁷ Now the Lord is the Spirit, and where the Spirit of the Lord is, there is liberty [emancipation from bondage, true freedom].

18 And we all, with unveiled face, continually seeing as in a mirror the glory of the Lord, are progressively being transformed into His image from [one degree of] glory to [even more] glory, which comes from the Lord, [who is] the Spirit.

CHAPTER 9

Eternal Life Is It for everyone?

O ne thing we need to understand is that each of us will live eternally. Whether it is in a state of happiness with God or in misery in Hell. We need to know how scripture provides insights into this. First there is the fact that the body will die or stop working. At this point our spirit and body separate. The memories of the acts and choices of our life carries with us. It is stored in a memory bank and this is where our judgement lies. You see we condemn ourselves by our choices and actions in this life. So, at the time our body dies the spirit separates from the body and stands before God. At that point God assigns a place for our spirits to reside until the final judgement and the resurrection of our body and spirit which will be rejoined as one forevermore. Then the final judgement occurs and the second death is granted to the those who choose not to accept God; along with eternal life to those written in the book of life.

REVELATION 20:1-15 KING JAMES VERSION (KJV)
¹ And I saw an angel come down from heaven, having the key of the bottomless pit and a great chain in his hand.
² And he laid hold on the dragon, that old serpent, which is the Devil, and Satan, and bound him a thousand years,
³ And cast him into the bottomless pit, and shut him up, and set a seal upon him, that he should deceive the nations no more, till the thousand years should be fulfilled: and after that he must be loosed a little season.
⁴ And I saw thrones, and they sat upon them, and judgment was given unto them: and I saw the souls of them that were beheaded for the witness of Jesus, and for the word of God, and which had

not worshipped the beast, neither his image, neither had received his mark upon their foreheads, or in their hands; and they lived and reigned with Christ a thousand years.

5 But the rest of the dead lived not again until the thousand years were finished. This is the first resurrection.

6 Blessed and holy is he that hath part in the first resurrection: on such the second death hath no power, but they shall be priests of God and of Christ, and shall reign with him a thousand years.

7 And when the thousand years are expired, Satan shall be loosed out of his prison,

8 And shall go out to deceive the nations which are in the four quarters of the earth, Gog, and Magog, to gather them together to battle: the number of whom is as the sand of the sea.

9 And they went up on the breadth of the earth, and compassed the camp of the saints about, and the beloved city: and fire came down from God out of heaven, and devoured them.

10 And the devil that deceived them was cast into the lake of fire and brimstone, where the beast and the false prophet are, and shall be tormented day and night for ever and ever.

11 And I saw a great white throne, and him that sat on it, from whose face the earth and the heaven fled away; and there was found no place for them.

12 And I saw the dead, small and great, stand before God; and the books were opened: and another book was opened, which is the book of life: and the dead were judged out of those things which were written in the books, according to their works.

13 And the sea gave up the dead which were in it; and death and hell delivered up the dead which were in them: and they were judged every man according to their works.

14 And death and hell were cast into the lake of fire. This is the second death.

15 And whosoever was not found written in the book of life was cast into the lake of fire.

At the final judgement we will be either assigned to live with God or sent to the lake of fire which is reserved for the devils and his angels and his followers. As scripture states here, we all will live eternally. Those who have chosen to accept Christ as their savior and have repented of not following the design in our conscience which is detailed in many different actions of individuals in scripture and consent to allow God through the Holy Spirit to transform us into the image of Christ (that is to think in right ways and learn to truly love in a Godly manner) are consigned to eternal punishment. So, the answer to the question do all have eternal life is no. Only those who have made the agreement in earnest will be allowed to share in this experience. Though it is God's will that we all accept His invitation to not perish. It is our choice to accept or reject the invitation to repent and accept Jesus as our savior which determines whether we will receive eternal life or continue to live in our sins in the place reserved for the rebellious or those who are evil. Evil does not suggest that someone has committed murder but evil is not living a life of righteousness. There a multitude of acts which are termed as evil in scripture. These are not limited to the seven things God hates in the lifestyle of men. Scripture lists these as follows:

PSALM 45:6-8 KING JAMES VERSION (KJV)

6 Thy throne, O God, is for ever and ever: the sceptre of thy kingdom is a right sceptre.

7 Thou lovest righteousness, and hatest wickedness: therefore God, thy God, hath anointed thee with the oil of gladness above thy fellows.

8 All thy garments smell of myrrh, and aloes, and cassia, out of the ivory palaces, whereby they have made thee glad.

DEUTERONOMY 12:30-32 KING JAMES VERSION (KJV)

30 Take heed to thyself that thou be not snared by following them, after that they be destroyed from before thee; and that thou enquire not after their gods, saying, How did these nations serve their gods? even so will I do likewise.

31 Thou shalt not do so unto the Lord thy God: for every abomination to the Lord, which he hateth, have they done unto their gods; for even their sons and their daughters they have burnt in the fire to their gods.

32 What thing soever I command you, observe to do it: thou shalt not add thereto, nor diminish from it.

MALACHI 2:15-17 KING JAMES VERSION (KJV)

15 And did not he make one? Yet had he the residue of the spirit. And wherefore one? That he might seek a godly seed. Therefore take heed to your spirit, and let none deal treacherously against the wife of his youth.

16 For the Lord, the God of Israel, saith that he hateth putting away: for one covereth violence with his garment, saith the Lord of hosts: therefore take heed to your spirit, that ye deal not treacherously.

17 Ye have wearied the Lord with your words. Yet ye say, Wherein have we wearied him? When ye say, Every one that doeth evil is good in the sight of the Lord, and he delighteth in them; or, Where is the God of judgment?

1 JOHN 4:19-21 KING JAMES VERSION (KJV)

[19] *We love him, because he first loved us.*

[20] *If a man say, I love God, and hateth his brother, he is a liar: for he that loveth not his brother whom he hath seen, how can he love God whom he hath not seen?*

[21] *And this commandment have we from him, That he who loveth God love his brother also.*

LEVITICUS 20:1-24 KING JAMES VERSION (KJV)

[1] *And the Lord spake unto Moses, saying,*

[2] *Again, thou shalt say to the children of Israel, Whosoever he be of the children of Israel, or of the strangers that sojourn in Israel, that giveth any of his seed unto Molech; he shall surely be put to death: the people of the land shall stone him with stones.*

[3] *And I will set my face against that man, and will cut him off from among his people; because he hath given of his seed unto Molech, to defile my sanctuary, and to profane my holy name.*

[4] *And if the people of the land do any ways hide their eyes from the man, when he giveth of his seed unto Molech, and kill him not:*

[5] *Then I will set my face against that man, and against his family, and will cut him off, and all that go a whoring after him, to commit whoredom with Molech, from among their people.*

[6] *And the soul that turneth after such as have familiar spirits, and after wizards, to go a whoring after them, I will even set my face against that soul, and will cut him off from among his people.*

[7] *Sanctify yourselves therefore, and be ye holy: for I am the Lord your God.*

[8] *And ye shall keep my statutes, and do them: I am the Lord which sanctify you.*

[9] *For every one that curseth his father or his mother shall be surely put to death: he hath cursed his father or his mother; his blood shall be upon him.*

[10] *And the man that committeth adultery with another man's wife, even he that committeth adultery with his neighbour's wife, the adulterer and the adulteress shall surely be put to death.*

[11] *And the man that lieth with his father's wife hath uncovered his father's nakedness: both of them shall surely be put to death; their blood shall be upon them.*

[12] *And if a man lie with his daughter in law, both of them shall surely be put to death: they have wrought confusion; their blood shall be upon them.*

¹³ If a man also lie with mankind, as he lieth with a woman, both of them have committed an abomination: they shall surely be put to death; their blood shall be upon them.

¹⁴ And if a man take a wife and her mother, it is wickedness: they shall be burnt with fire, both he and they; that there be no wickedness among you.

¹⁵ And if a man lie with a beast, he shall surely be put to death: and ye shall slay the beast.

¹⁶ And if a woman approach unto any beast, and lie down thereto, thou shalt kill the woman, and the beast: they shall surely be put to death; their blood shall be upon them.

¹⁷ And if a man shall take his sister, his father's daughter, or his mother's daughter, and see her nakedness, and she see his nakedness; it is a wicked thing; and they shall be cut off in the sight of their people: he hath uncovered his sister's nakedness; he shall bear his iniquity.

¹⁸ And if a man shall lie with a woman having her sickness, and shall uncover her nakedness; he hath discovered her fountain, and she hath uncovered the fountain of her blood: and both of them shall be cut off from among their people.

¹⁹ And thou shalt not uncover the nakedness of thy mother's sister, nor of thy father's sister: for he uncovereth his near kin: they shall bear their iniquity.

²⁰ And if a man shall lie with his uncle's wife, he hath uncovered his uncle's nakedness: they shall bear their sin; they shall die childless.

²¹ And if a man shall take his brother's wife, it is an unclean thing: he hath uncovered his brother's nakedness; they shall be childless.

²² Ye shall therefore keep all my statutes, and all my judgments, and do them: that the land, whither I bring you to dwell therein, spue you not out.

²³ And ye shall not walk in the manners of the nation, which I cast out before you: for they committed all these things, and therefore I abhorred them.

²⁴ But I have said unto you, Ye shall inherit their land, and I will give it unto you to possess it, a land that floweth with milk and honey: I am the Lord your God, which have separated you from other people.

PROVERBS 6:14-21 KING JAMES VERSION (KJV)

¹⁴ Frowardness is in his heart, he deviseth mischief continually; he soweth discord.

¹⁵ Therefore shall his calamity come suddenly; suddenly shall he be broken without remedy.

[16] *These six things doth the Lord hate: yea, seven are an abomination unto him:*

[17] *A proud look, a lying tongue, and hands that shed innocent blood,*

[18] *An heart that deviseth wicked imaginations, feet that be swift in running to mischief,*

[19] *A false witness that speaketh lies, and he that soweth discord among brethren.*

[20] *My son, keep thy father's commandment, and forsake not the law of thy mother:*

[21] *Bind them continually upon thine heart, and tie them about thy neck.*

PSALM 81:14-15 AMPLIFIED BIBLE (AMP)

[14] *"Then I would quickly subdue and humble their enemies*
And turn My hand against their adversaries;

[15] *Those who hate the Lord would pretend obedience to Him and cringe before Him,*
And their time of punishment would be forever.

PROVERBS 1:28-33 KING JAMES VERSION (KJV)

[28] *Then shall they call upon me, but I will not answer; they shall seek me early, but they shall not find me:*

[29] *For that they hated knowledge, and did not choose the fear of the Lord:*

[30] *They would none of my counsel: they despised all my reproof.*

[31] *Therefore shall they eat of the fruit of their own way, and be filled with their own devices.*

[32] *For the turning away of the simple shall slay them, and the prosperity of fools shall destroy them.*

[33] *But whoso hearkeneth unto me shall dwell safely, and shall be quiet from fear of evil.*

Summary

PROVERBS 1:20-33 AMPLIFIED BIBLE (AMP)

Wisdom Warns

[20] *[a]Wisdom shouts in the street,*
She raises her voice in the markets;

[21] *She calls out at the head of the noisy streets [where large crowds gather];*
At the entrance of the city gates she speaks her words:

[22] *"How long, O naive ones [you who are easily misled], will you love being simple-minded and undiscerning?*

How long will scoffers [who ridicule and deride] delight in scoffing,
How long will fools [who obstinately mock truth] hate knowledge?
23 "If you will turn and pay attention to my rebuke,
Behold, I [Wisdom] will pour out my spirit on you;
I will make my words known to you.
24 "Because I called and you refused [to answer],
I stretched out my hand and no one has paid attention [to my offer];
25 And you treated all my counsel as nothing
And would not accept my reprimand,
26 I also will laugh at your disaster;
I will mock when your dread and panic come,
27 When your dread and panic come like a storm,
And your disaster comes like a whirlwind,
When anxiety and distress come upon you [as retribution].
28 "Then they will call upon me (Wisdom), but I will not answer;
They will seek me eagerly but they will not find me,
29 Because they hated knowledge
And did not choose the fear of the Lord [that is, obeying Him with
reverence and awe-filled respect],
30 They would not accept my counsel,
And they spurned all my rebuke.
31 "Therefore they shall eat of the fruit of their own [wicked] way
And be satiated with [the penalty of] their own devices.
32 "For the turning away of the [b]naive will kill them,
And the careless ease of [self-righteous] fools will destroy them.
33 "But whoever listens to me (Wisdom) will live securely and in
confident trust
And will be at ease, without fear or dread of evil."
Footnotes:
Proverbs 1:20 Wisdom is personified as a woman in vv 20-33 and
speaks, in the first person, of godly wisdom. Read the word
"wisdom" as "the wisdom of God" and see the wonderful power of
this book.
Proverbs 1:32 Lit simple ones.

The bible is full of these types of statements showing God makes the offer of eternal life to all but because of their refusal to accept it He cannot provide it so their choice is eternal punishment. So eternal life is only provided to those who accept it. Those who don't accept it choose eternal punishment to their dismay. Be careful for there are those who teach all will be saved (universal salvation) which is a lie of the devil just as he deceived Eve in the garden when he got her to question God's decree that she would surely die. Yes, we cannot just quote John 3:16 and stop there. We have to continue on with verses 17 through 21 and then we have the whole picture not just what makes us feel good. Let's end this one with the following scriptures.

PROVERBS 8:12-14 KING JAMES VERSION (KJV)

12 I wisdom dwell with prudence, and find out knowledge of witty inventions.

13 The fear of the Lord is to hate evil: pride, and arrogancy, and the evil way, and the froward mouth, do I hate.

14 Counsel is mine, and sound wisdom: I am understanding; I have strength.

JOHN 3:1-21 AMPLIFIED BIBLE (AMP)

The New Birth

1 Now there was a certain man among the Pharisees named Nicodemus, a ruler (member of the Sanhedrin) among the Jews,

2 who came to Jesus at night and said to Him, "Rabbi (Teacher), we know [without any doubt] that You have come from God as a teacher; for no one can do these signs [these wonders, these attesting miracles] that You do unless God is with him."

3 Jesus answered him, "I assure you and most solemnly say to you, unless a person is born again [reborn from above—spiritually transformed, renewed, sanctified], he cannot [ever] see and experience the kingdom of God."

4 Nicodemus said to Him, "How can a man be born when he is old? He cannot enter his mother's womb a second time and be born, can he?"

5 Jesus answered, "I assure you and most solemnly say to you, unless one is born of water and the Spirit he cannot [ever] enter the kingdom of God.

6 That which is born of the flesh is flesh [the physical is merely physical], and that which is born of the Spirit is spirit.

7 Do not be surprised that I have told you, 'You must be born again [reborn from above—spiritually transformed, renewed, sanctified].'

8 The wind blows where it wishes and you hear its sound, but you do not know where it is coming from and where it is going; so it is with everyone who is born of the Spirit."

9 Nicodemus said to Him, "How can these things be possible?"

10 Jesus replied, "You are the [great and well-known] teacher of Israel, and yet you do not know nor understand these things [from Scripture]?

11 I assure you and most solemnly say to you, we speak only of what we [absolutely] know and testify about what we have [actually] seen [as eyewitnesses]; and [still] you [reject our evidence and] do not accept our testimony.

12 If I told you earthly things [that is, things that happen right here on earth] and you do not believe, how will you believe and trust Me if I tell you heavenly things?

13 No one has gone up into heaven, but there is One who came down from heaven, the Son of Man [Himself—whose home is in heaven].

14 Just as Moses lifted up the [bronze] serpent in the desert [on a pole], so must the Son of Man be lifted up [on the cross],

15 so that whoever believes will in Him have eternal life [after physical death, and will actually live forever].

16 "For God so [greatly] loved and dearly prized the world, that He [even] gave His [One and] [a]only begotten Son, so that whoever believes and trusts in Him [as Savior] shall not perish, but have eternal life.

17 For God did not send the Son into the world to judge and condemn the world [that is, to initiate the final judgment of the world], but that the world might be saved through Him.

18 Whoever believes and has decided to trust in Him [as personal Savior and Lord] is not judged [for this one, there is no judgment, no rejection, no condemnation]; but the one who does not believe [and has decided to reject Him as personal Savior and Lord] is judged already [that one has been convicted and sentenced], because [b]he has not believed and trusted in the name of the [One and] only begotten Son of God [the One who is truly unique, the only One of His kind, the One who alone can save him].

19 This is the judgment [that is, the cause for indictment, the test by which people are judged, the basis for the sentence]: the Light has come into the world, and people loved the [c]darkness rather than the Light, for their deeds were evil.

20 For every wrongdoer hates the Light, and does not come to the Light [but shrinks from it] for fear that his [sinful, worthless] activities will be exposed and condemned.

21 But whoever practices truth [and does what is right—morally, ethically, spiritually] comes to the Light, so that his works may be plainly shown to be what they are—accomplished in God [divinely prompted, done with God's help, in dependence on Him]."

Footnotes:

John 3:16 Jesus, God's only Son, the One who is truly unique, the only one of His kind.

John 3:18 The Greek refers to an unsaved person who has made the decision not to believe in the Son, Jesus Christ, that is, not to accept the salvation offered by the Son and commit to follow Him. Such a person stands condemned by God unless he changes his mind.

John 3:19 See note 1:5.

CHAPTER 10

Eternal Life is it a Goal We should Seek For?

Is eternal life what we should seek for? First of all, it is not we who seek it. It is God who seeks to provide this to those who wish to accept it. No, it is not of our effort but it is the will and provision of God to offer this to all who will accept His offer to receive it. It the goal of all those who have accepted the invitation and it is granted to us just as we receive an honorary diploma from a university that we did not earn by meeting the requirement to attend the classes but it is earned out of consideration of God's love for us. Unlike a degree we earn through years of study and achieving proficiency first He provides the instruction and implants the knowledge in compliance with our wishes to serve and Him and accept adoption of His righteousness in us. It is a reversal of the process we are used to in humanistic learning where we have to study and memorize theories. In His offer He offers to implant His ideas and plans and procedures within us as we allow Him to do so or when we are ready to accept them and to allow them to replace our old ideas and ways of acting them out. So, for those who have accepted His offer we are granted the gift of eternal life immediately. We have to be told that we have to seek His ways as part of our way of living doing and thinking to be aware of our part in the process. Some do not realize that eternal life is a sequence of relearning of that which is in our conscience God has provided His programmed design of right and wrong and to allow Him to make this part of our makeup so as to be acceptable to Him. They believe it is a work of theirs but it is not. It is a work performed by Him with our cooperation. When we ask for Him to show us what is there about us that is unacceptable He will show these to us as we are ready to handle them and then we have to make the choice to release these from controlling our conduct and to replace them with the right way to perform in accordance with His original design.

For those who desire to stand in His presence it is desirable above all things. This is because He cannot stand the minutest area of sin in His presence. This is exemplified in a couple of parables Jesus told. One is the man who found a treasure in a field and sold all he had so that he could purchase the field. The other is the parable of the young man who came to Him and asked what must He do to gain eternal life. Here they are for you to study and meditate on.

MATTHEW 13:43-50 KING JAMES VERSION (KJV)

[43] Then shall the righteous shine forth as the sun in the kingdom of their Father. Who hath ears to hear, let him hear.

[44] Again, the kingdom of heaven is like unto treasure hid in a field; the which when a man hath found, he hideth, and for joy thereof goeth and selleth all that he hath, and buyeth that field.

[45] Again, the kingdom of heaven is like unto a merchant man, seeking goodly pearls:

[46] Who, when he had found one pearl of great price, went and sold all that he had, and bought it.

[47] Again, the kingdom of heaven is like unto a net, that was cast into the sea, and gathered of every kind:

[48] Which, when it was full, they drew to shore, and sat down, and gathered the good into vessels, but cast the bad away.

[49] So shall it be at the end of the world: the angels shall come forth, and sever the wicked from among the just,

[50] And shall cast them into the furnace of fire: there shall be wailing and gnashing of teeth.

MATTHEW 6:20-22 KING JAMES VERSION (KJV)

[20] But lay up for yourselves treasures in heaven, where neither moth nor rust doth corrupt, and where thieves do not break through nor steal:

[21] For where your treasure is, there will your heart be also.

[22] The light of the body is the eye: if therefore thine eye be single, thy whole body shall be full of light.

MARK 10:15-30 KING JAMES VERSION (KJV)

[15] *Verily I say unto you, Whosoever shall not receive the kingdom of God as a little child, he shall not enter therein.*

[16] *And he took them up in his arms, put his hands upon them, and blessed them.*

[17] *And when he was gone forth into the way, there came one running, and kneeled to him, and asked him, Good Master, what shall I do that I may inherit eternal life?*

[18] *And Jesus said unto him, Why callest thou me good? there is none good but one, that is, God.*

[19] *Thou knowest the commandments, Do not commit adultery, Do not kill, Do not steal, Do not bear false witness, Defraud not, Honour thy father and mother.*

[20] *And he answered and said unto him, Master, all these have I observed from my youth.*

[21] *Then Jesus beholding him loved him, and said unto him, One thing thou lackest: go thy way, sell whatsoever thou hast, and give to the poor, and thou shalt have treasure in heaven: and come, take up the cross, and follow me.*

[22] *And he was sad at that saying, and went away grieved: for he had great possessions.*

[23] *And Jesus looked round about, and saith unto his disciples, How hardly shall they that have riches enter into the kingdom of God!*

[24] *And the disciples were astonished at his words. But Jesus answereth again, and saith unto them, Children, how hard is it for them that trust in riches to enter into the kingdom of God!*

[25] *It is easier for a camel to go through the eye of a needle, than for a rich man to enter into the kingdom of God.*

[26] *And they were astonished out of measure, saying among themselves, Who then can be saved?*

[27] *And Jesus looking upon them saith, With men it is impossible, but not with God: for with God all things are possible.*

[28] *Then Peter began to say unto him, Lo, we have left all, and have followed thee.*

[29] *And Jesus answered and said, Verily I say unto you, There is no man that hath left house, or brethren, or sisters, or father, or mother, or wife, or children, or lands, for my sake, and the gospel's,*

[30] *But he shall receive an hundredfold now in this time, houses, and brethren, and sisters, and mothers, and children, and lands, with persecutions; and in the world to come eternal life.*

So many today expect that hundred-fold return on their investment. They don't realize that the return lies in caring for the widows and orphans and providing for the poor. This is where we gain wives and children and houses and lands. It is through the ministry we provide to those in need. We are one family in Christ so all His children are our children and all He has he provides to us.

MATTHEW 25:40-46 KING JAMES VERSION

40 And the King shall answer and say unto them, Verily I say unto you, Inasmuch as ye have done it unto one of the least of these my brethren, ye have done it unto me.

41 Then shall he say also unto them on the left hand, Depart from me, ye cursed, into everlasting fire, prepared for the devil and his angels:

42 For I was an hungred, and ye gave me no meat: I was thirsty, and ye gave me no drink:

43 I was a stranger, and ye took me not in: naked, and ye clothed me not: sick, and in prison, and ye visited me not.

44 Then shall they also answer him, saying, Lord, when saw we thee an hungred, or athirst, or a stranger, or naked, or sick, or in prison, and did not minister unto thee?

45 Then shall he answer them, saying, Verily I say unto you, Inasmuch as ye did it not to one of the least of these, ye did it not to me.

46 And these shall go away into everlasting punishment: but the righteous into life eternal.

Summary

D o you desire to live with God or to die in sin? This is our choice. We can choose life with God in joy, peace and happiness with a revised nature or we choose a life of eternal torment with our sins in misery. In my mind I see that we should all desire eternal life with all our sins forgiven with a new start and no sin residing in us.

ACTS 18:24-26 KING JAMES VERSION

24 And a certain Jew named Apollos, born at Alexandria, an eloquent man, and mighty in the scriptures, came to Ephesus.

25 This man was instructed in the way of the Lord; and being fervent in the spirit, he spake and taught diligently the things of the Lord, knowing only the baptism of John.

26 And he began to speak boldly in the synagogue: whom when Aquila and Priscilla had heard, they took him unto them, and expounded unto him the way of God more perfectly.

ROMANS 12:10-12 KING JAMES VERSION

[10] Be kindly affectioned one to another with brotherly love; in honour preferring one another;

[11] Not slothful in business; fervent in spirit; serving the Lord;

[12] Rejoicing in hope; patient in tribulation; continuing instant in prayer;

COLOSSIANS 4:11-13 KING JAMES VERSION

[11] And Jesus, which is called Justus, who are of the circumcision. These only are my fellowworkers unto the kingdom of God, which have been a comfort unto me.

[12] Epaphras, who is one of you, a servant of Christ, saluteth you, always labouring fervently for you in prayers, that ye may stand perfect and complete in all the will of God.

[13] For I bear him record, that he hath a great zeal for you, and them that are in Laodicea, and them in Hierapolis.

JAMES 5:10-17 KING JAMES VERSION

[10] Take, my brethren, the prophets, who have spoken in the name of the Lord, for an example of suffering affliction, and of patience.

[11] Behold, we count them happy which endure. Ye have heard of the patience of Job, and have seen the end of the Lord; that the Lord is very pitiful, and of tender mercy.

[12] But above all things, my brethren, swear not, neither by heaven, neither by the earth, neither by any other oath: but let your yea be yea; and your nay, nay; lest ye fall into condemnation.

[13] Is any among you afflicted? let him pray. Is any merry? let him sing psalms.

[14] Is any sick among you? let him call for the elders of the church; and let them pray over him, anointing him with oil in the name of the Lord:

[15] And the prayer of faith shall save the sick, and the Lord shall raise him up; and if he have committed sins, they shall be forgiven him.

[16] Confess your faults one to another, and pray one for another, that ye may be healed. The effectual fervent prayer of a righteous man availeth much.

[17] Elias was a man subject to like passions as we are, and he prayed earnestly that it might not rain: and it rained not on the earth by the space of three years and six months.

1 PETER 4:7-9 KING JAMES VERSION

[7] But the end of all things is at hand: be ye therefore sober, and watch unto prayer.

[8] And above all things have fervent charity among yourselves: for charity shall cover the multitude of sins.

⁹ Use hospitality one to another without grudging.

2 PETER 3:11-13 KING JAMES VERSION

¹¹ Seeing then that all these things shall be dissolved, what manner of persons ought ye to be in all holy conversation and godliness,

¹² Looking for and hasting unto the coming of the day of God, wherein the heavens being on fire shall be dissolved, and the elements shall melt with fervent heat?

¹³ Nevertheless we, according to his promise, look for new heavens and a new earth, wherein dwelleth righteousness.

DEUTERONOMY 11:12-14 KING JAMES VERSION

¹² A land which the Lord thy God careth for: the eyes of the Lord thy God are always upon it, from the beginning of the year even unto the end of the year.

¹³ And it shall come to pass, if ye shall hearken diligently unto my commandments which I command you this day, to love the Lord your God, and to serve him with all your heart and with all your soul,

¹⁴ That I will give you the rain of your land in his due season, the first rain and the latter rain, that thou mayest gather in thy corn, and thy wine, and thine oil.

1 SAMUEL 12:23-25 KING JAMES VERSION

²³ Moreover as for me, God forbid that I should sin against the Lord in ceasing to pray for you: but I will teach you the good and the right way:

²⁴ Only fear the Lord, and serve him in truth with all your heart: for consider how great things he hath done for you.

²⁵ But if ye shall still do wickedly, ye shall be consumed, both ye and your king.

JOEL 2:11-13 KING JAMES VERSION

¹¹ And the Lord shall utter his voice before his army: for his camp is very great: for he is strong that executeth his word: for the day of the Lord is great and very terrible; and who can abide it?

¹² Therefore also now, saith the Lord, turn ye even to me with all your heart, and with fasting, and with weeping, and with mourning:

¹³ And rend your heart, and not your garments, and turn unto the Lord your God: for he is gracious and merciful, slow to anger, and of great kindness, and repenteth him of the evil.

We can see from these scriptures that we are to fervently and with all-purpose seek after the Lord which is our allowing the work of Holy Spirit to transform us into the likeness of Jesus. The word of scripture which emphasizes "seek ye first the kingdom of God, which is eternal life" that that pleasing the Lord should be the first priority. Our priority should be to do what we need to do on this earth for our bodies to survive but in accordance with the goal of eternal life uppermost in everything we do.

MATTHEW 6:30-34 KING JAMES VERSION

30 Wherefore, if God so clothe the grass of the field, which to day is, and to morrow is cast into the oven, shall he not much more clothe you, O ye of little faith?

31 Therefore take no thought, saying, What shall we eat? or, What shall we drink? or, Wherewithal shall we be clothed?

32 (For after all these things do the Gentiles seek:) for your heavenly Father knoweth that ye have need of all these things.

33 But seek ye first the kingdom of God, and his righteousness; and all these things shall be added unto you.

34 Take therefore no thought for the morrow: for the morrow shall take thought for the things of itself. Sufficient unto the day is the evil thereof.

Repent of those things which are called to our attention by the Holy Spirit and allow God to fix the wrong and make it right. We are to be ever aware of the work of the Holy Spirit and do all things to honor God and not ourselves. This is the goal of fasting which we should always be doing. Isn't fasting and prayer the act of focusing on God while doing the everyday tasks of life. Is it not recognizing no matter what we do we should put God first and His righteousness? In our church we have been provided specific words to pray as a part of our commitment in taking communion. These are as follows:

SECTION 17 DOCTRINE & COVENANTS

[Sec 17:22a] It is expedient that the church meet together often to partake of bread and wine in remembrance of the Lord Jesus;

[Sec 17:22b] and the elder or priest shall administer it; and after this manner shall he administer it:

[Sec 17:22c] He shall kneel with the church and call upon the Father in solemn prayer, saying,

[Sec 17:22d] O God, the eternal Father, we ask thee in the name of thy Son Jesus Christ, to bless and sanctify this bread to the souls of all those who partake of it, that they may eat in remembrance of the body of thy Son, and witness unto thee, O God, the eternal Father, that they are willing to take upon them the name of thy Son, and always remember him and keep his commandments

which he has given them, that they may always have his Spirit to be with them.
Amen.
[Sec 17:23a] The manner of administering the wine: He shall take the cup also, and say:
[Sec 17:23b] O God, the eternal Father, we ask thee in the name of thy Son Jesus Christ, to bless and sanctify this wine to the souls of all those who drink of it, that they may do it in remembrance of the blood of thy Son which was shed for them, that they may witness unto thee, O God, the eternal Father, that they do always remember him, that they may have his Spirit to be
with them. Amen.

You see we are to commit to the commandments of Christ in all that we do and to be mindful of the fact we need the Holy Spirit and that are attention should always be aware of His sacrifice and our appreciation through the acceptance of the work of the Holy Spirit to transform us into His image which is for us to come to the point where we as Jesus did do nothing unless we have comprehended that this is the way God does it. These prayers point out that we can choose to follow or not follow the Holy Spirit. In order for us to glorify God we need to be involved in doing things in His design and patterns for all things to fit in place as He made. All things have a specific set of rules, or criteria or boundaries in which they operate in. If you don't follow these things then the result will be that it will go wrong and the desired result is not produced.

CHAPTER 11

Why God Wants Us in Eternity

W
e see from the book of Genesis that God saw what he made and it was declared good. He produced order in the creation and this He did for the benefit of the whole. Each part complimenting the other.

GENESIS 1:1-30 KING JAMES VERSION

¹ In the beginning God created the heaven and the earth.

² And the earth was without form, and void; and darkness was upon the face of the deep. And the Spirit of God moved upon the face of the waters.

³ And God said, Let there be light: and there was light.

⁴ And God saw the light, that it was good: and God divided the light from the darkness.

⁵ And God called the light Day, and the darkness he called Night. And the evening and the morning were the first day.

⁶ And God said, Let there be a firmament in the midst of the waters, and let it divide the waters from the waters.

⁷ And God made the firmament, and divided the waters which were under the firmament from the waters which were above the firmament: and it was so.

⁸ And God called the firmament Heaven. And the evening and the morning were the second day.

⁹ And God said, Let the waters under the heaven be gathered together unto one place, and let the dry land appear: and it was so.

¹⁰ And God called the dry land Earth; and the gathering together of the waters called he Seas: and God saw that it was good.

¹¹ And God said, Let the earth bring forth grass, the herb yielding seed, and the fruit tree yielding fruit after his kind, whose seed is in itself, upon the earth: and it was so.

¹² And the earth brought forth grass, and herb yielding seed after his kind, and the tree yielding fruit, whose seed was in itself, after his kind: and God saw that it was good.

¹³ And the evening and the morning were the third day.

¹⁴ And God said, Let there be lights in the firmament of the heaven to divide the day from the night; and let them be for signs, and for seasons, and for days, and years:

¹⁵ And let them be for lights in the firmament of the heaven to give light upon the earth: and it was so.

¹⁶ And God made two great lights; the greater light to rule the day, and the lesser light to rule the night: he made the stars also.

¹⁷ And God set them in the firmament of the heaven to give light upon the earth,

¹⁸ And to rule over the day and over the night, and to divide the light from the darkness: and God saw that it was good.

¹⁹ And the evening and the morning were the fourth day.

²⁰ And God said, Let the waters bring forth abundantly the moving creature that hath life, and fowl that may fly above the earth in the open firmament of heaven.

²¹ And God created great whales, and every living creature that moveth, which the waters brought forth abundantly, after their kind, and every winged fowl after his kind: and God saw that it was good.

²² And God blessed them, saying, Be fruitful, and multiply, and fill the waters in the seas, and let fowl multiply in the earth.

²³ And the evening and the morning were the fifth day.

²⁴ And God said, Let the earth bring forth the living creature after his kind, cattle, and creeping thing, and beast of the earth after his kind: and it was so.

²⁵ And God made the beast of the earth after his kind, and cattle after their kind, and every thing that creepeth upon the earth after his kind: and God saw that it was good.

²⁶ And God said, Let us make man in our image, after our likeness: and let them have dominion over the fish of the sea, and over the fowl of the air, and over the cattle, and over all the earth, and over every creeping thing that creepeth upon the earth.

²⁷ So God created man in his own image, in the image of God created he him; male and female created he them.

28 And God blessed them, and God said unto them, Be fruitful, and multiply, and replenish the earth, and subdue it: and have dominion over the fish of the sea, and over the fowl of the air, and over every living thing that moveth upon the earth.

29 And God said, Behold, I have given you every herb bearing seed, which is upon the face of all the earth, and every tree, in the which is the fruit of a tree yielding seed; to you it shall be for meat.

30 And to every beast of the earth, and to every fowl of the air, and to every thing that creepeth upon the earth, wherein there is life, I have given every green herb for meat: and it was so.

So, one reason is that God choose man to compliment Himself. This is identified the statement that God made man in His image. This goes to show that He created man to be like Him and to emulate Himself.

GENESIS 1:26-28 KING JAMES VERSION

26 And God said, Let us make man in our image, after our likeness: and let them have dominion over the fish of the sea, and over the fowl of the air, and over the cattle, and over all the earth, and over every creeping thing that creepeth upon the earth.

27 So God created man in his own image, in the image of God created he him; male and female created he them.

28 And God blessed them, and God said unto them, Be fruitful, and multiply, and replenish the earth, and subdue it: and have dominion over the fish of the sea, and over the fowl of the air, and over every living thing that moveth upon the earth.

No other part of His creation was endowed with this attribute. He singled out man and Him only to have the ability to resemble Him in all respects. You see God is one God made up of the trinity Father Son and Holy Spirit. They work as one walking in agreement at all times so that there is a seamless connection between them. Man was created to seamlessly fit into this relationship sharing all the good aspects of His character and abilities, up the point of being the one in charge.

You see when He called the universe into being, He had one goal to make it prefect. He thought through each detail and when things were as he wanted, He made them to the specifications in which they are to exist in. We can see this in our solar system. Each planet has a specific set of parameters which they follow. They each have a specific size and orbit around the sun in a predetermined pattern. Each planet has a dependency on each other to stay in their prescribed orbits. The sun provides the light and heat needed for each one of these planets to exist. It produces the necessary light and heat each planet needs. Yet all the solar system has as its source an invisible force which controls it. We call this gravity. But what is it that provides the energy for them to constantly circle the sun? What put them in motion in the first place. Where did that energy come from? Yes, God produced this in beginning and as we can see each planet keeps moving around and around with nothing visible providing the push they need to keep moving around the sun and staying in their prescribed orbits. We have learned from observing God's creation that it takes energy to put something into motion and to keep it moving. We know we need to refuel a car for it to get where we want it to go. Such is God's creation. It all depends on His energy to keep it doing what it was created to do.

As we find in scripture it is by the power of God we live and move and have our being. He is the source of energy which keeps us going or living.

He created our bodies to depend on some other form of life to live. The food sources are necessary for our bodies to continue to live. We depend on some other part of the creation to die in order for our bodies to function and continue to work in their designed realm. When we eat the body takes the nutrients and the fuel supplied by the food source to continue to live. Yet there is some invisible thing implanted in us which determines that even though our bodies have the ability to continually regenerate, they grow old and wear down.

ACTS 17:27-29 KING JAMES VERSION
[27] That they should seek the Lord, if haply they might feel after him, and find him, though he be not far from every one of us:
[28] For in him we live, and move, and have our being; as certain also of your own poets have said, For we are also his offspring.
[29] Forasmuch then as we are the offspring of God, we ought not to think that the Godhead is like unto gold, or silver, or stone, graven by art and man's device.

PSALM 136:24-26 KING JAMES VERSION
[24] And hath redeemed us from our enemies: for his mercy endureth for ever.
[25] Who giveth food to all flesh: for his mercy endureth for ever.
[26] O give thanks unto the God of heaven: for his mercy endureth for ever.

So apart from God we cannot exist. So, he made us with an intercedence on Him for us to exist. We are part of Him in such a way that we cannot exist apart from Him. Just as the sun provides the necessary light and heat each planet needs to exist and stay in their prescribed orbits, He provides for us the needed basis for our life.

ACTS 17:27-29 KING JAMES VERSION

²⁷ That they should seek the Lord, if haply they might feel after him, and find him, though he be not far from every one of us:

²⁸ For in him we live, and move, and have our being; as certain also of your own poets have said, For we are also his offspring.

²⁹ Forasmuch then as we are the offspring of God, we ought not to think that the Godhead is like unto gold, or silver, or stone, graven by art and man's device.

When you consider how are bodies are made it is a remarkable number of pieces which all function one purpose which is our existence. Each part serves a different function. Yet the one goal for each one is to provide all that is needed for our physical existence. As a matter of fact, we all have an interconnectivity that we cannot seem to do without.

EPHESIANS 4:15-17 KING JAMES VERSION

¹⁵ But speaking the truth in love, may grow up into him in all things, which is the head, even Christ:

¹⁶ From whom the whole body fitly joined together and compacted by that which every joint supplieth, according to the effectual working in the measure of every part, maketh increase of the body unto the edifying of itself in love.

¹⁷ This I say therefore, and testify in the Lord, that ye henceforth walk not as other Gentiles walk, in the vanity of their mind,

1 CORINTHIANS 12:10-31 KING JAMES VERSION

¹⁰ To another the working of miracles; to another prophecy; to another discerning of spirits; to another divers kinds of tongues; to another the interpretation of tongues:

¹¹ But all these worketh that one and the selfsame Spirit, dividing to every man severally as he will.

¹² For as the body is one, and hath many members, and all the members of that one body, being many, are one body: so also is Christ.

¹³ For by one Spirit are we all baptized into one body, whether we be Jews or Gentiles, whether we be bond or free; and have been all made to drink into one Spirit.

¹⁴ For the body is not one member, but many.

¹⁵ If the foot shall say, Because I am not the hand, I am not of the body; is it therefore not of the body?

16 And if the ear shall say, Because I am not the eye, I am not of the body; is it therefore not of the body?

17 If the whole body were an eye, where were the hearing? If the whole were hearing, where were the smelling?

18 But now hath God set the members every one of them in the body, as it hath pleased him.

19 And if they were all one member, where were the body?

20 But now are they many members, yet but one body.

21 And the eye cannot say unto the hand, I have no need of thee: nor again the head to the feet, I have no need of you.

22 Nay, much more those members of the body, which seem to be more feeble, are necessary:

23 And those members of the body, which we think to be less honourable, upon these we bestow more abundant honour; and our uncomely parts have more abundant comeliness.

24 For our comely parts have no need: but God hath tempered the body together, having given more abundant honour to that part which lacked.

25 That there should be no schism in the body; but that the members should have the same care one for another.

26 And whether one member suffer, all the members suffer with it; or one member be honoured, all the members rejoice with it.

27 Now ye are the body of Christ, and members in particular.

28 And God hath set some in the church, first apostles, secondarily prophets, thirdly teachers, after that miracles, then gifts of healings, helps, governments, diversities of tongues.

29 Are all apostles? are all prophets? are all teachers? are all workers of miracles?

30 Have all the gifts of healing? do all speak with tongues? do all interpret?

31 But covet earnestly the best gifts: and yet shew I unto you a more excellent way.

When a baby comes into this world it will not continue to live without experiencing human touch and compassion. If left alone even though it may have food water and air to breathe it will die just because it does not sense the warmth of being wanted or sense that others are part of them. The need for other human interaction is built within us until we choose to do without it.

Summary

Essentially it all comes down to the fact that God loves His creation. It is not His desire that any of it perish but He will not allow it to continue to suffer either if something is not right. Everything God does is based on the fact that above all else He loves all things. Just as stated in Genesis when it states how when He created each part of His creation, He said it was good. And in so many other places in scripture it identifies His loving attributes. That is why we find so many names for Him in the scripture. In so many instances people have identified Him with a specific attribute of love so the names just keep compiling. It is not that God only performs love in isolated ways it is just we perceive it as the need which we have at this time is met. So, when He healed someone, they named Him Jehovah My Healer.

EXODUS 15:26 KING JAMES VERSION
26 And said, If thou wilt diligently hearken to the voice of the Lord thy God, and wilt do that which is right in his sight, and wilt give ear to his commandments, and keep all his statutes, I will put none of these diseases upon thee, which I have brought upon the Egyptians: for I am the Lord that healeth thee.

This is from Jehovah Rapha in the Septuagint.

When He fulfilled the exact need for something, they named Him Jehovah My Provider.

GENESIS 22:14 KING JAMES VERSION
14 And Abraham called the name of that place Jehovahjireh: as it is said to this day, In the mount of the Lord it shall be seen.

When He saved someone from harm, He became Jehovah My Deliverer and so on and so forth. In each instance it is the same God yet we categorize Him based on our limited understanding of Who He is and what love is. You see God's love is wholistic. That is why He terms Himself as I Am. He is all that you need anytime you call upon Him and trust Him to fulfill any need you have at any time. He performs these acts every day for everyone and yet we only prescribe them to special occasions.

GENESIS 15:1-3 KING JAMES VERSION
1 After these things the word of the Lord came unto Abram in a vision, saying, Fear not, Abram: I am thy shield, and thy exceeding great reward.

² And Abram said, Lord God, what wilt thou give me, seeing I go childless, and the steward of my house is this Eliezer of Damascus? ³ And Abram said, Behold, to me thou hast given no seed: and, lo, one born in my house is mine heir.

EXODUS 3:13-15 KING JAMES VERSION

¹³ And Moses said unto God, Behold, when I come unto the children of Israel, and shall say unto them, The God of your fathers hath sent me unto you; and they shall say to me, What is his name? what shall I say unto them?

¹⁴ And God said unto Moses, I Am That I Am: and he said, Thus shalt thou say unto the children of Israel, I Am hath sent me unto you.

¹⁵ And God said moreover unto Moses, Thus shalt thou say unto the children of Israel, the Lord God of your fathers, the God of Abraham, the God of Isaac, and the God of Jacob, hath sent me unto you: this is my name for ever, and this is my memorial unto all generations.

That is why when we invent our own gods. We make one to cover each individual need. Just as in the time of Jesus people had so many different idols to cover every different need they had in their lives in which they needed assistance beyond their perceived capabilities. There is only one true God and we need to recognize this. He and He alone created us and sustains us. Or maybe I should say they (the Godhead or the trinity) has done these things. I am led to close this section with the words from John 3:16-21.

JOHN 3:16-21 KING JAMES VERSION

¹⁶ For God so loved the world, that he gave his only begotten Son, that whosoever believeth in him should not perish, but have everlasting life.

¹⁷ For God sent not his Son into the world to condemn the world; but that the world through him might be saved.

¹⁸ He that believeth on him is not condemned: but he that believeth not is condemned already, because he hath not believed in the name of the only begotten Son of God.

¹⁹ And this is the condemnation, that light is come into the world, and men loved darkness rather than light, because their deeds were evil.

²⁰ For every one that doeth evil hateth the light, neither cometh to the light, lest his deeds should be reproved.

²¹ But he that doeth truth cometh to the light, that his deeds may be made manifest, that they are wrought in God.

CHAPTER 12

What Part We Have in Eternity

We are to share the ability to, one bypass the second death and two to be acceptable to God in accordance with the degree we accept the regeneration of our spiritual life in accordance with the work of the Holy Spirit in this life. Then there are those who have not had the opportunity to accept the work of Christ in this life but have walked in obedience with the preprogrammed instruction set within us (we call this our conscience) and accept Jesus in the life to come. We see this in the scripture when we are told how Jesus went to paradise and preached to them.

LUKE 23:35-44 KING JAMES VERSION (KJV)
35 And the people stood beholding. And the rulers also with them derided him, saying, He saved others; let him save himself, if he be Christ, the chosen of God.
36 And the soldiers also mocked him, coming to him, and offering him vinegar,
37 And saying, If thou be the king of the Jews, save thyself.
38 And a superscription also was written over him in letters of Greek, and Latin, and Hebrew, This Is The King Of The Jews.
39 And one of the malefactors which were hanged railed on him, saying, If thou be Christ, save thyself and us.
40 But the other answering rebuked him, saying, Dost not thou fear God, seeing thou art in the same condemnation?
41 And we indeed justly; for we receive the due reward of our deeds: but this man hath done nothing amiss.
42 And he said unto Jesus, Lord, remember me when thou comest into thy kingdom.

⁴³ And Jesus said unto him, Verily I say unto thee, Today shalt thou be with me in paradise.

⁴⁴ And it was about the sixth hour, and there was a darkness over all the earth until the ninth hour.

MATTHEW 12:39-41 KING JAMES VERSION (KJV)

³⁹ But he answered and said unto them, An evil and adulterous generation seeketh after a sign; and there shall no sign be given to it, but the sign of the prophet Jonas:

⁴⁰ For as Jonas was three days and three nights in the whale's belly; so shall the Son of man be three days and three nights in the heart of the earth.

⁴¹ The men of Nineveh shall rise in judgment with this generation, and shall condemn it: because they repented at the preaching of Jonas; and, behold, a greater than Jonas is here.

1 PETER 3:18-20 KING JAMES VERSION (KJV)

¹⁸ For Christ also hath once suffered for sins, the just for the unjust, that he might bring us to God, being put to death in the flesh, but quickened by the Spirit:

¹⁹ By which also he went and preached unto the spirits in prison;

²⁰ Which sometime were disobedient, when once the longsuffering of God waited in the days of Noah, while the ark was a preparing, wherein few, that is, eight souls were saved by water.

Those who have not had an opportunity to accept Jesus in this life too but would have if provided the opportunity will be allowed the same privileges as those who accepted Jesus and His sacrifice for them on this earth. This is why Jesus taught that the payment for those who came in the last hour will be the same as those who were hired from the beginning in the parable of the hired workers and their pay.

MATTHEW 20:1-16 KING JAMES VERSION (KJV)

¹ For the kingdom of heaven is like unto a man that is an householder, which went out early in the morning to hire labourers into his vineyard.

² And when he had agreed with the labourers for a penny a day, he sent them into his vineyard.

³ And he went out about the third hour, and saw others standing idle in the marketplace,

⁴ And said unto them; Go ye also into the vineyard, and whatsoever is right I will give you. And they went their way.

⁵ Again he went out about the sixth and ninth hour, and did likewise.

⁶ And about the eleventh hour he went out, and found others standing idle, and saith unto them, Why stand ye here all the day idle?

⁷ They say unto him, Because no man hath hired us. He saith unto them, Go ye also into the vineyard; and whatsoever is right, that shall ye receive.

⁸ So when even was come, the lord of the vineyard saith unto his steward, Call the labourers, and give them their hire, beginning from the last unto the first.

⁹ And when they came that were hired about the eleventh hour, they received every man a penny.

¹⁰ But when the first came, they supposed that they should have received more; and they likewise received every man a penny.

¹¹ And when they had received it, they murmured against the goodman of the house,

¹² Saying, These last have wrought but one hour, and thou hast made them equal unto us, which have borne the burden and heat of the day.

¹³ But he answered one of them, and said, Friend, I do thee no wrong: didst not thou agree with me for a penny?

¹⁴ Take that thine is, and go thy way: I will give unto this last, even as unto thee.

¹⁵ Is it not lawful for me to do what I will with mine own? Is thine eye evil, because I am good?

¹⁶ So the last shall be first, and the first last: for many be called, but few chosen.

Summary

So, what is our role. The work is being done by God and Jesus but our part is to accept the free gift and to repent allowing the Holy Spirit to convert us into the image of Christ Jesus so that we will not just bear a physical resemblance but a spiritual one.

EPHESIANS 2:8-10 KING JAMES VERSION (KJV)

⁸ For by grace are ye saved through faith; and that not of yourselves: it is the gift of God:

⁹ Not of works, lest any man should boast.

¹⁰ For we are his workmanship, created in Christ Jesus unto good works, which God hath before ordained that we should walk in them.

We have it easy for as Jesus says His burden is easy. That is because we cannot perform anything which will make us perfect in the sight of God except to admit that He and Christ Jesus are God and to allow them to work the work of perfection in us.

DEUTERONOMY 12:8-10 KING JAMES VERSION (KJV)

8 Ye shall not do after all the things that we do here this day, every man whatsoever is right in his own eyes.

9 For ye are not as yet come to the rest and to the inheritance, which the Lord your God giveth you.

10 But when ye go over Jordan, and dwell in the land which the Lord your God giveth you to inherit, and when he giveth you rest from all your enemies round about, so that ye dwell in safety;

ISAIAH 45:19-25 KING JAMES VERSION (KJV)

19 I have not spoken in secret, in a dark place of the earth: I said not unto the seed of Jacob, Seek ye me in vain: I the Lord speak righteousness, I declare things that are right.

20 Assemble yourselves and come; draw near together, ye that are escaped of the nations: they have no knowledge that set up the wood of their graven image, and pray unto a god that cannot save.

21 Tell ye, and bring them near; yea, let them take counsel together: who hath declared this from ancient time? who hath told it from that time? have not I the Lord? and there is no God else beside me; a just God and a Saviour; there is none beside me.

22 Look unto me, and be ye saved, all the ends of the earth: for I am God, and there is none else.

23 I have sworn by myself, the word is gone out of my mouth in righteousness, and shall not return, That unto me every knee shall bow, every tongue shall swear.

24 Surely, shall one say, in the Lord have I righteousness and strength: even to him shall men come; and all that are incensed against him shall be ashamed.

25 In the Lord shall all the seed of Israel be justified, and shall glory.

1 JOHN 1:8-9 KING JAMES VERSION (KJV)

8 If we say that we have no sin, we deceive ourselves, and the truth is not in us.

9 If we confess our sins, he is faithful and just to forgive us our sins, and to cleanse us from all unrighteousness.

LUKE 5:31-33 KING JAMES VERSION (KJV)

31 And Jesus answering said unto them, They that are whole need not a physician; but they that are sick.

32 I came not to call the righteous, but sinners to repentance.

³³ And they said unto him, Why do the disciples of John fast often, and make prayers, and likewise the disciples of the Pharisees; but thine eat and drink?

³⁴ And he said unto them, Can ye make the children of the bridechamber fast, while the bridegroom is with them?

³⁵ But the days will come, when the bridegroom shall be taken away from them, and then shall they fast in those days.

Post Script

I would like to ask a favor of you. I would appreciate it if you would provide an honest evaluation of this book and post it on my Facebook page for this book and if you have an Amzon.com account please add it there also. If you wish I would also like your permission to share your comments with others.

Appendix

Scripture References

About the Author

Lorenzo Hill and his wife Clotilde right after marriage, 1969

Lorenzo Hill and his wife Clotilde after 49 years, 2018
We have now been married 52 years as of 2020

Lorenzo Hill has served in the ministry of the Community of Christ (formerly The Reorganized Church of Jesus Christ Of Latter Day Saints) since 1976, when he was ordained a priest. Throughout his ministry, he has been a self-supporting minister. He has served in his current office of Evangelist since 1988 and continues to be very active in ministry, serving in various roles of leadership and other roles in which he is called to serve. His passion has been providing guidance to youth. He had to sadly stop this part of his ministry for health reasons. He provides ongoing ministry through his commitment to spreading word in preaching and bringing ministry to the sick in soul and body.

Lorenzo was raised in St. Louis Missouri and resided there until he received his Bachelor of Science degree in Chemical Engineering in 1970 from the University of Missouri at Rolla (currently known as the Missouri School of Science and Technology). He is a registered retired professional engineer. He has worked in the petroleum industry since he graduated from college and has retired twice. Needless to say, he has moved around quite a bit. He has been blessed to be able to see many other countries because of his employment and for pleasure. The Holy Spirit has used this to open his eyes to the suffering that many experiences in this life due to governmental policies and personal lifestyles.

He has been married to his wife, Clotilde for 49 years. She has been his constant support in all his endeavors. They have three children: two daughters; Alicia Renee Hill, Reynada Charlese Robinson, and one son; Jared Lorenzo Hill.

Although he has taken many post graduate courses in both engineering and ministry, Lorenzo chose not to pursue an advanced degree. He has written numerous technical reports and technical texts for the training and instruction of engineers and construction inspectors. All of these works, however, were prepared for either clients or for internal company use and as such, were not issued as external publications.

He was inspired to publish two books prior to this endeavor. These books are titled:
Formulas In The Scripture
E =MC2
THE KEY TO OUR PENTECOST EXPERIENCE.

AND

What God Intends for Us in His Commandments
What we can gain from God's commandments
    AND
What God is Saying in the Book of Revelation:
    PART 1 :
DO WE BELIEVE GOD IS AND HIS WORD IS TRUE?

These works are currently in print and can be purchased on Amazon.com in paperback or e-book format.

If there is one way to express His walk with Christ there are some words from a hymn in our church entitled Admonition. These are as follows:

"Grace waits upon the souls who try"

As Paul states I am not perfect yet, but I strive for the high calling of Christ Jesus and await the transformation to be like Him in all ways. Thanks to my wife and daughters for assisting in these works. Praise be to God for His inspiring spirit, enlightenment and encouragement. It is by God's grace I have been allowed to present His intent and purposes in these books so that we may all know the truth of the Gospel.

www.ingramcontent.com/pod-product-compliance
Lightning Source LLC
LaVergne TN
LVHW021500080426
835509LV00018B/2351